D0728441

Praise for *Living for Another*

"Scripture contains almost sixty 'one-another' passages, yet many believers may be unable to name even a handful, much less live them out. In *Living for Another*, Brent Gambrell builds a biblical case for selfless living before outlining a plan for serving others. Real-world experiences coupled with a candid sense of humor make this book accessible to read and easy to implement. You will want to pass this book on to a friend after you read it."
—**ROBBY GALLATY**, Senior Pastor, Long Hollow Baptist Church, author of *Growing Up* and *The Forgotten Jesus*

"As a professional golfer, my life sets me up for always chasing 'another.' I want another birdie that could mean another low round that could lead to another win. I want to win another major, another Ryder Cup, and no matter how much I achieve, I'm left wanting more. Brent's book, *Living for Another*, is a poignant reminder of which 'another' I should be chasing. He does a beautiful job of illustrating the fullness of a life that is emptied of self and lived for another. That's a life I want."
—**ZACH JOHNSON**, twelve-time PGA Tour Champion

"Brent is a master at making the theologically complex undeniably simple. In *Living for Another*, he explains the true heart of the Christian life. I was amazed at how much ground he was able to cover and how convicted he was able to make me feel in such a short amount of time. If you're currently obsessed with yourself, and you don't want to change, please don't read this book."
—**MIKE DONEHEY**, singer, Tenth Avenue North

"Our culture has it so backwards when we seek happiness by looking out for ourselves. I'm so excited for people to read

Living for Another and to learn that God's plan leads to joy when we live a life focused on others!"

—JONNY DIAZ, contemporary Christian artist

"If you want to understand one-anothering, Brent Gambrell's book, *Living for Another*, is a must read. A question I ask is, 'What do you think Jesus meant when He said Go?' *Another* will show you."

—DR. DOUG DEES, Associate Pastor of Education and Equipping, First Moore Baptist Church, Moore, Oklahoma

"Having dealt with so many Christians who lose the joy of their walk, *Living for Another* answers the why as well as what to do. Brent Gambrell reminds us to be a funnel and not a puddle in our walk. I am excited to see how God uses this book to impact lives."

—Youth Evangelism Strategist, State Convention of Baptists

LIVING FOR

ANOTHER

MORE OF OTHERS

LESS OF YOU

BRENT GAMBRELL

ABINGDON PRESS
NASHVILLE

LIVING FOR ANOTHER
MORE OF OTHERS, LESS OF YOU

Copyright © 2017 by Abingdon Press

All rights reserved.

No part of this work may be reproduced or transmitted in any form or by any means, electronic or mechanical, including photocopying and recording, or by any information storage or retrieval system, except as may be expressly permitted by the 1976 Copyright Act or in writing from the publisher. Requests for permission can be addressed to Permissions, The United Methodist Publishing House, 2222 Rosa L. Parks Blvd., PO Box 280988, Nashville, TN, 37228-0988 or e-mailed to permissions@umpublishing.org.

Library of Congress Cataloging-in-Publication Data has been requested.
ISBN 978-1-5018-4184-2

Unless otherwise indicated, all Scripture quotations are from The Holy Bible, English Standard Version® (ESV®), copyright © 2001 by Crossway, a publishing ministry of Good News Publishers. Used by permission. All rights reserved.

Scripture quotations marked (KJV) are taken from The Authorized (King James) Version. Rights in the Authorized Version in the United Kingdom are vested in the Crown. Reproduced by permission of the Crown's patentee, Cambridge University Press.

Scripture quotations marked (NIV) are taken from the Holy Bible, New International Version®, NIV®. Copyright © 1973, 1978, 1984, 2011 by Biblica, Inc.™ Used by permission of Zondervan. All rights reserved worldwide. www.zondervan .com. The "NIV" and "New International Version" are trademarks registered in the United States Patent and Trademark Office by Biblica, Inc.™

Scripture quotations marked "NKJV™" are taken from the New King James Version®. Copyright © 1982 by Thomas Nelson, Inc. Used by permission. All rights reserved.

17 18 19 20 21 22 23 24 25—10 9 8 7 6 5 4 3 2 1
MANUFACTURED IN THE UNITED STATES OF AMERICA

CONTENTS

ACKNOWLEDGMENTS

Writing this book started so long ago, I'm ashamed to admit it. In fact, there was actually *another* book begun and put aside in the middle of writing *Another*. This book would not be sitting in front of you if not for the prayers, prodding, and support of some amazing people in my life.

First, I must thank Cathy Bell. To say she merely assisted and typed what you see here would be a lie. (Many times she didn't even type what I dictated because "I don't like what you said.") You rock, lady!

To the incredible staff at BGM/A Door to Hope—Misty, Lisa, Kelly, Matt, and our board of directors—whose support and patience have gone far above what a ministry team should be asked to supply, I love you all.

I also owe so much to Julie Breihan, Dawn Woods, and the team at Abingdon Press for not telling me that I write like an infant and to walk away from the crayon!

There is *another* that was and is always my biggest fan

and the best research assistant a guy could ask for: my mom Jeannette Gambrell. Thanks for all the ways you've invested in me.

Last, I need to thank all the people who have poured into me through teaching, preaching, books, blogs, and even posts and Tweets throughout my Christian walk. In fact, there may be thoughts and lessons in this writing that are uncited but were passed to me from you and I simply can't remember who shared them with me through the years. I promise I'll cite you if we reprint! Know that I am just the compiled sum of all you have spoken into my life. Thanks.

This book is dedicated to Glenn Gambrell, my late father, to Lon Slechta, and to all those quiet, sometimes silent servants who, through their humble, selfless lives, have unknowingly taught, inspired, and even shamed the rest of us into pouring ourselves out for those around us.

INTRODUCTION

When Solomon said, "of making many books there is no end" (Ecclesiastes 12:12b), he was saying to beware because there will always be another book on every topic. I hope this isn't just another book. My prayer has been that this book is simply a look at another kind of life, a life lived for *another*.

Many people feel like they merely take up space on this earth while others really live! I believe I really began living when I started to understand that God's intent was for me to pour myself out completely for the sake of the gospel and for those He puts in my path.

Now, I am no expert in the Christian life. In fact, I don't want to be. In my experience, most experts are boring. There is also a tendency to believe that experts have arrived at some destination where they now possess "the truth" about a given topic. I never intend to stand as an expert on top of an invisible pyramid and tell anyone how to be more like me. You don't know me. You don't want that! The fact is,

I am totally unqualified to write a book on living a selfless life. Like most of us, my motives are never completely pure. I think of myself more than others many times, and I must repent of the desires that my selfish flesh screams for every day. But I have learned that one of the amazing gifts God gives His kids is this: He makes the unworthy, worthy. Though I don't always live it myself, I can give you the following encouragement. I've had the privilege of walking alongside a few people who truly live out their lives in selfless service to others and I've grown through my "holy envy." I want that kind of life, a life of adventure, a life that impacts others like those servants have impacted mine. I hope you want to come on this adventure, too.

Just know this, it may sound a bit obvious, but this book is not the answer to your problems, God is. When reading a book or hearing a good message, I often find myself inspired and excited that I have learned a truth new to me. The problems begin when I try to "park" on that truth and make it the central theme in my spiritual growth. I heard an old preacher once say, "When *a truth* becomes *the truth*, God will make it an *untruth*." He will allow everything to break down because He knows that He is the only truth that lasts. My prayer is that you see our time together as an opportunity to draw near to Him and not just as some life lesson to be learned. Ask God for His perspective on your life, relationships, and attitudes; be open for Him to transform you into a clearer reflection of His son, the ultimate template for our lives.

So What / Now What?

A book, a message, or a teaching is like sunscreen—if it stays in the container, it does you no good. You need to apply it personally, or that awesome new revelation is completely useless. I don't know about you, but I must also re-apply constantly as needed (and I need it more than I would like to admit). With this knowledge of myself, I decided to place a section at the end of each chapter to help answer the question "So what?" What am I to do with these truths in my everyday walk? There is also an optional "Now what?" activity to help you further absorb what you are applying.

These questions are not meant to have one right answer. Many of these questions have been designed to make you think about your life and generate your own answers. They were not written to prompt simple regurgitation of the statements in the chapter. Take the time to allow God to reach into your heart and change your mind about your life and your purpose. My prayer is that these times of reflection will draw you closer to Christ and lead you to become a more selfless and servant-minded person. The questions in the "So what?" sections can be used in a small group setting as well as in personal meditation and reflection.

I hope these sections help guide you in the process of "fleshing out" *another* life.

WHAT IS ANOTHER LIFE?

Chapter One

ME FIRST

Let no one seek his own good, but the good of his neighbor.
1 Corinthians 10:24

I f I just lived in ANOTHER place...
   If only I had ANOTHER boss/teacher/body/personality, I would be happy...
   If only I had ANOTHER spouse/job/car/piece of cake, my life would be complete...
   This is the mantra of the modern world.
   On the surface, these complaints seem to be expressions of this generation's blatant materialism, envy, or greed. So Christian leaders, with good intentions, have preached against, written about, bound, and rebuked this problem of one's selfishness, of always wanting "another." But the problem remains, doesn't it? Why? Because we see "another" as merely an adjective describing our problem and not the problem itself. Obviously, we have ANOTHER problem.

You see, within that one word is both the problem *and* the answer. This is how *Dictionary.com* defines *another*:

> *Another*: (adjective) different; distinct; of a different period, place, or kind; (pronoun) a person other than oneself or the one specified.

Pay special attention to what *another* means when it's used as an adjective: "different; distinct, of a different period, place, or kind." Therein lies the problem…and it began with Adam and Eve.

God said to Adam and Eve, "You have everything here in this garden I made for you. I freely give all this abundance to you simply because I love you and want to pamper you with grace. There is one tree I do not want you to eat from, but all the rest, everything else you see, is for you." But they wanted more. God's provision and abundance was not enough. They looked around at all that bounty but chose to focus on the one thing God said they couldn't have and to believe the lie Satan told them that they could be like God.

> So when the woman saw that the tree was good for food, and that it was a delight to the eyes, and that the tree was to be desired to make one wise, she took of its fruit and ate, and she also gave some to her husband who was with her, and he ate. (Genesis 3:6)

They wanted something "different," something they thought was better…something other. They wanted anything other than what they already possessed in Eden. *In*

Eden! And the desire for "something else" has warped and destroyed the souls of men and women since.

There is ANOTHER way.

In contrast to many self-help books of our day that focus on improving oneself, finding oneself, and getting the most potential out of oneself, I want to explore the possibility of another way, *another* life; the kind of life that does not revolve around self at all. Instead, it is a life poured out for another.

There it is. Did you catch it? The answer to the void in our lives is in the second definition of the word. The pronoun *another* refers to "a person other than oneself."

I believe the "abundant life" that Jesus spoke of in John 10:10—"I came that they may have life and have it abundantly"—must be attainable in this life or surely He would have told us He was speaking of the next life in heaven. The question becomes: What does the abundant life look like here on earth and how do we define that life? Jesus offers us a ticket to heaven, and that is a tremendous gift, one to be received with gratitude. But so many people focus on that aspect that they miss the gifts Jesus is offering us in this life. The abundant life that Jesus offers us is the peace, fulfillment, and direction here on earth. It is the confidence that comes from being a child of the King with an eternal inheritance.

We receive two things at our salvation: forgiveness and grace. We don't just receive forgiveness for our sin, but God also forgives us for the sacrifice of His Son. He forgives us not just for the sins we commit but also for our sin that sent His Son to the cross. That gift in itself would be enough to fulfill our lives, but God goes further by also offering us grace. Grace is this: we now receive the inheritance of His Son. We get all His "stuff." At our salvation, we received the righteousness of Jesus as a gift. We got His love, His wisdom, His strength, and so on. His authority is ours. We received His eternal life. That is abundant!

However, there seems to be a paradox in how we walk in this abundant life. Jesus's remarkable statement about how we can follow "His" way is found in Matthew 16:25: "For whoever would save his life will lose it, but whoever loses his life for my sake will find it."

This amazing life that Jesus was describing surprisingly requires a life of voluntary loss, a life depleted intentionally. He refined His statement when He condensed the Ten Commandments for His followers: "Love the Lord your God with all your heart and with all your soul and with all your mind....Love your neighbor as yourself" (Matthew 22:37, 39). He was teaching us to pour ourselves out to *God* and to *others*, and promising that when we do this, we will have all we need.

In 2 Peter 1:3, Peter tells us that "His divine power has granted to us all things that pertain to life and godliness." It is clear that our Creator would better know what we need than even we comprehend. I believe His will is to abundantly provide for our physical, spiritual, and emotional needs, and He knows the path to get to that place of fulfillment. That path is a selfless path of pouring out our life. He even said of Himself: "The Son of Man came not to be served but to serve, and to give his life as a ransom for many" (Matthew 20:28).

His life was not spent for self at all but for another. For us.

This begs the questions: How are you spending your life? For *whom* are you spending it? Somewhere within your answers is the abundant life.

The God-Shaped Hole

There is a "God-shaped" hole in humans
that only He can fill.

This evangelistic cliché carries with it deep truths that are sometimes overlooked. God, in His infinite wisdom, inhabited Adam at his creation when He breathed His Spirit into that lump of clay. At that moment, Adam was complete and fulfilled in his body, soul, and spirit (see 1 Thessalonians 5:23), but it didn't take long before Adam sinned by reaching for something *other* than what he had. When Adam committed that first sin, it severed the intimate relationship that existed between God and him, leaving behind a definite *hole* in Adam. We all feel the consequences, and only the Spirit of God can fill the empty space in our hearts. God's Spirit is the only piece that will fit in the "puzzle" and fill the void. Jesus did just that. On the cross, Jesus declared, "It

7

is finished!" His sacrifice and the resurrection that He knew was coming completed the work of salvation and opened up the way for the Holy Spirit to come. The hole no longer had to exist in our hearts and once He "moves in" at our salvation, that hole is never empty again.

But salvation for the believer is also a beginning. The apostle Paul in Romans 6:6 taught that the "old self" is crucified with Christ and we become a new creation. Our old life is gone, and when we accept Jesus's sacrifice and love, we are given another life; one that is directed, empowered, and complete. But though complete in Christ, the believer often begins to feel a new and distinct unease in his or her spirit. It is a "soul deep" yearning for something more, something else that "feels" like another hole or void.

During my years of speaking and working with churches, universities, and student ministries, many Christians have approached me with the same question. Adults tend to flower it up with spiritual-sounding phrases: "How do I reach the next dispensation of God's grace?" Students tend to just say what they feel: "How do I get to the next level?" or "Why am I still empty?"

It's all the same question: they are expressing the desire for *something else*. They want something more, something better…something different. We all have the same hole, and we all try to fill this hole with stuff, experiences, Bible studies, busyness…the list goes on. The problem is those "things" will never fulfill us.

I think we all can agree that there is an obvious reason

why lost people feel there is a "hole" inside of them. They are in desperate need of Christ *in* them. This need leads to the question, "Why, then, does a Christian feel such a void, such a longing?" It's because Christ's life within us compels us to seek something more than just the ticket into heaven. We know that another life awaits us in eternity, but what about now? The yearning for more springs from this: "I am the vine; you are the branches" (John 15:5).

Growing up in Central Florida, I was surrounded by orange groves. I also had many friends and family who worked within the citrus industry, so over the years I unwittingly learned a little about these trees. Most people may not know that many of the orange trees that produce the sweetest fruit aren't one tree at all; each tree is actually two trees. Most trees that produce sweet fruit aren't hardy enough to survive the short cold snaps Florida experiences each winter (that's right, kids; it gets cold in Florida too—sometimes) or the insects. So when the sapling is young, the grower grafts or "buds" the weak variety into the root of a "sour stock" tree. These sour trees produce bitter oranges if left to grow alone. However, when they are budded with a sweet orange branch, a tree is produced that has the best qualities of both trees. Sometimes many varieties of oranges can be grafted into the rootstock of one tree. This produces the strength of the sour stock and the many flavors of the other varieties in one tree.

This process also works within the grape industry. For centuries, vineyards worldwide have used vine-grafting to produce the best fruit. You see, these farmers prosper because they know this truth: when grafted into the vine, what is true about the vine is also true about the branches.

When you accepted Christ and became a Christian, you were "grafted into the vine." That vine is Christ. Now you are in Him and He is in you (see John 15:1-4). The results of this grafting are not only your salvation but also this awesome new reality: what is true about the Vine is now true about you! The Vine's life flows through you!

The Bible puts it like this: "Christ who *is* your life…" (Colossians 3:4, emphasis added) will complement all aspects of your life. Therefore:

Christ's life is your life—*you're in the vine.*

Christ's strength is your strength—*you're in the vine.*

Christ's peace is your peace—*you're in the vine.*

Christ's joy is your joy—*you're in the vine.*

And here is the answer to the soul-deep yearning we experience: what satisfies Christ will be the only thing that satisfies you because *you're in the vine*!

So What Satisfies Christ?

Jesus was sitting with His followers one day when they came to Him and said, "Rabbi, eat" (John 4:31).

He replied, "I have food to eat that you do not know about" (John 4:32).

His disciples were confused (as they often were). Had someone brought Him something to eat?

That's when Jesus revealed an incredible revelation that

goes unseen or experienced by the average Christian. He said, "My *food* is to do the will of him who sent me and to accomplish his work" (John 4:34, emphasis added).

Wow!

The two things that were His food, His sustenance, the things that fulfilled and satisfied Jesus were:

1. to do the will of the Father, and

2. to finish the Father's work.

Even as a child, this was the driving force behind Christ's life. In one of the only accounts of His youth, Jesus and His earthly parents went to Jerusalem to celebrate the feast of Passover. When the feast was over, Mary and Joseph left for home, but Jesus went missing. After an exhaustive search, they found their twelve-year-old in the temple courts listening, learning, and even teaching!

I am sure Joseph and Mary, in that moment, weren't inclined to "spare the rod" on Jesus. However, they were stopped in their tracks by His beautiful yet baffling excuse: "Why did you seek Me? Did you not know that I must be about My Father's business?" (Luke 2:49 NKJV). How can you argue with that? Jesus was showing us that His life was all about the Father's business. So what is the Father's business? The "will of God" and His "work that needs to be finished" is this: to redeem mankind and to glorify Himself.

His life is now our life, and what is true about the Vine is now true about us.

11

In Ephesians 1, Paul unpacks God's predestined plan for mankind. Paul explains we were given the "Holy Spirit, who is the guarantee of our inheritance until we acquire possession of it, to the praise of his glory" (vv. 13–14).

Redeem: to make the "most" of.
Glorify: to make big; to acknowledge and draw attention to His greatness.

Jesus saw the culmination of His life's purpose fulfilled at the cross when the redemption of humankind was finally made possible and God was most glorified. This same Jesus now lives in each one of us, the redeemed. His life is now our life, and what is true about the Vine is now true about us. You see, we will never be truly satisfied until our lives are all about "the Father's business."

Just like Jesus, we are most fulfilled when we:

1. **do the will of the Father** by
   helping redeem another or
   making the most of the people
   He puts in our path, and

2. **finish the work** by bringing
   glory to God.

We don't need another thing. We have all we need when we live our lives for everyone other than ourselves.

This Is "Another Life"!

How can we stay "fresh" and alive in our walk with Christ? I have a great illustration to explain how this "another" life keeps us from growing stale and leaving us weary.

There are two great seas in the Middle East: the Sea of Galilee and the Dead Sea. Both sit in the path of and are fed by the Jordan River. The Galilee and its surrounding land is one of the most fertile places on the earth. The land produces many varieties of crops such as bananas, citrus fruits, olives, grapes, and wheat. There is also an abundant fishing industry in its fresh waters for tilapia, catfish, sardines, and other river life. In contrast, almost nothing grows in or around the Dead Sea. It is described as a bleak and arid desert. There is little rainfall in this area. Only minuscule quantities of bacteria live here. Why is there such a difference between the two? The life-giving Jordan feeds them both, but the difference is this: the Jordan flows into the Galilee and out the other side. Then it flows on to the Dead Sea, but there is no outlet from there. It just stops. The water stays and stagnates there.

This is a truth we can live by! The reason many Christians dry up and stagnate in their Christian walk is that although they may be actively going to church and having the Word poured into them on a weekly or daily basis, they are not pouring out anywhere! So their walk becomes drudgery, or it comes to a halt and they wonder why.

You see, you were made to live your life as a funnel, not

a puddle! As God gives to us, we are to funnel everything to others. Only then will we see living water flow through us to nourish the world around us. When we allow Jesus (and His love, mercy, and forgiveness) to pour through us and out to others, we will *never* become dry or stagnant. Jesus explained this clearly in John 7:38: "Whoever believes in me, as the Scripture has said, 'Out of his heart *will flow* rivers of living water'" (emphasis added). We are *not* to just hold His Spirit, His love, and the truths He reveals to us for just ourselves. We are to let it all spill out of us, letting the life-giving waters nourish those around us.

What does this mean for us? It means that while discipleship and our personal growth are critical, we cannot stop there, or even that knowledge will slip away. Yes, we need education in our churches today, but what we need more of is *revelation*! Revelation comes when we see God move in us, around us, and through us.

This funnel philosophy of living stands diametrically opposed to the kind of life the world would have us live. It is not a life of "me and mine." That worldview has led to generations of bored, childish, adrenaline junkies, and real junkies who are all looking for the next big thing, the next new adventure that never fulfills. A. W. Tozer was expressing this to his generation as well when he said, "The truly spiritual man is indeed something of an oddity. He lives not for himself but to promote the interests of Another."[1] His thoughts still apply to us today...on steroids!

Me First?

Before we can begin to unpack what *Another Life* looks like, we first need to examine ourselves. I know I sound like I am contradicting myself. Hang in there with me. Because the truth is, in order to solve your selfish problem, you've got to look at yourself first. But if that's where you stop, then you are going to be stuck in a life-smothering place that will not bring healing for yourself, nor will you be of any good to anyone else.

Every year millions of dollars are spent on therapy and self-help books. Feel free to "help yourself" to all those books that are guaranteed to help you fix yourself. Simply looking at yourself and picking yourself apart will not "fix" you because you'll be overlooking one thing: most of our problems are grounded in self! The Bible says that the flesh exalts it*self* (see 2 Corinthians 10:3-5). If it is going to do that, everything has to revolve around "me," my *flesh*.

Looking again at the fall of Adam may shed some light here. When God created Adam, His Spirit entered Adam, and there began a holy partnership and an unparalleled intimacy. They were mutually devoted to each other. Then, tempted by Satan, Adam and Eve committed that first great act of selfishness, wanting more than God had provided for them. Thus began Adam and Eve's downward spiral of self-preservation, self-gratification, and "me-centric" idolatry. And we have continued down the rabbit hole of sin and self.

The idolatry of "me" has destroyed people since Adam

and Eve. Judas's tragic life is one example of this truth. I've heard many different theories as to why Judas betrayed Jesus: for political gain, because of religious zealousness. But the truth is, the only motivation that Scripture gives us for Judas's actions is that he did it for the money (see Luke 22:4-6). He did it to benefit him*self*. Maybe we just don't want the motive to be that simple. Maybe we want his reasons to be more sinister so he won't remind us of ourselves quite so much.

But Judas should remind us of ourselves, because like him, we are all selfish. Anyone who has had the pleasure of raising a child will quickly tell you that from the womb, children are selfish. A comedian once said that when her child learned how to talk and really communicate, the first thing she wanted to ask was, "What did you want? You just kept crying! Really…what did you want?" From the very beginning, babies want their needs met their way.

My nephew learned how to manipulate everyone within his first week of life. I was visiting my sister and her husband to meet this new addition to our family. The baby had just eaten, had a clean diaper, and was comfortable and warm, but he wanted something else: attention from his mama. He seemed to know that if he cried, he would get exactly what he wanted. I would be holding him and he was completely fine, but when his mother was distracted and not paying attention to him, he would emit sounds as if I were pinching him! I remember laughing, shaking my head, and telling this newborn he was a "little liar." Yes, we are born in sin and are selfish from the very start.

Flesh

*Throughout our life, all of us battle our
selfish "me monster": the flesh.*

The flesh exalts itself and tries to make everything else
exalted as well. Think of someone you know who has bad
self-esteem. They have what the late Bill Gillham, founder of
Lifetime Ministries, termed "yucky flesh."[2] Have you noticed
that negative comments a person says about another person,
and negative circumstances in one's life, create "yucky flesh"?
Everything reinforces that negative self-image. A simple disagreement at work can send someone into the spiral of "everyone thinks I'm stupid; no one respects me." This tragic person subliminally demands that everyone around him or her
bow to this yucky flesh in order to fix the problem. Someone
like this can rarely maintain a mutually giving relationship
because it becomes a needy, one-sided affair.

The same can be said for those with an inflated self-
esteem. If you have this "U.S.D.A. Choice Select Cut Flesh,"
then everyone and everything in your life is used to boost
that image of self. Everything in your life has to bow down
to the altar of your *self*.

Our solutions to these "self" problems usually involve
an attempt to tinker with our flesh to make it better. We
are told by "experts" to follow "the six laws of..." or "the
twenty-eight surefire strategies to..." These "solutions" ultimately result in failure.

Paul presumably wrote thirteen books in the New Testament. Surely a man with that much wisdom from God would have figured out how to tinker with his flesh and fix it if it were possible. Instead, Paul said, "For I know that in me (that is, in my flesh) nothing good dwells" (Romans 7:18 NKJV). Paul told us, instead, to die to our flesh, to crucify the deeds of the flesh. He died daily to his flesh—to his selfish wants and needs. Paul lived for Christ and, in the process, learned the ultimate healing lifestyle: "to live is Christ, and to die is gain" (Philippians 1:21).

Consider Others

This book is the result of my years of counseling and mentoring and was truly birthed when a gentleman who came to my office began to describe in painstaking detail *all* the issues in his life, starting from his early years to his present relationship problems, work/boss issues, appearance, personality…the list went on and on. When he was finished discussing himself, I employed a tactic I had learned from author and counselor Michael Wells. I paused in silence for the uncomfortable but expected evaluation period. Then I said, "You're right. Your life really does stink! In fact," I continued, "if I had to think about you all day long, I would be depressed too!"

Now, before you think that I was too harsh and throw this book down, I also said, "If I had to think about *me* all day long, I would be depressed too!" My solution? I don't think about me; I consider others.

This man wanted me to dig into his past with him. He wanted (for the five hundredth time) to do some self-evaluation and soul searching for a few months and then have some epiphany that would reveal the truth that would miraculously heal him (which would likely only lead to a new cycle of evaluation, soul searching, and epiphany seeking to fix the next issue in the queue). To his great disappointment, I said, "Let's just skip to the end!"

Yes, there are times in counseling when we need to tread in the shallows of self for a bit. But let me state what is, for some, a revolutionary comment here. As someone who has been through counseling himself and is a proponent of good biblically based therapy, I can reveal this shocking truth: the best reason to study ourselves for any length time at all is to GET OVER OURSELVES!

In case you think I'm the first one to come up with this revolutionary philosophy, consider the wisdom of this commonly spoken prayer:

Peace Prayer of Saint Francis

> Lord, make me an instrument of your peace:
> where there is hatred, let me sow love;
> where there is injury, pardon;
> where there is doubt, faith;
> where there is despair, hope;
> where there is darkness, light;
> where there is sadness, joy.

O divine Master, grant that I may not so much seek
to be consoled as to console,
to be understood as to understand,
to be loved as to love.
For it is in giving that we receive,
it is in pardoning that we are pardoned,
and it is in dying that we are born to eternal life.
Amen.

Through the years, I have seen many people go through therapy, and it can be incredibly helpful for people. But I will always warn of the risk of becoming a chronic counselee.

I believe the goal of good counseling should be:

1. To know yourself—your past, present, and the trajectory of your future.

2. To identify false beliefs and faulty, destructive behavior patterns.

3. With God's guidance, to seek healing and make course corrections.

4. To focus on others instead of yourself.

As I've watched many people go through effective counseling, the most beautiful thing to see is when healed souls begin to use what they have learned to help other people, often those dealing with the same issues they have overcome. Their lives become illustrations of the biblical truth: "You meant evil against me, but God meant it for good" (Genesis 50:20). (We'll unpack this concept of healing in chapter 3.)

I do believe that a time of self-evaluation is very important before we can effectively give our lives to others. In fact, I think Jesus Himself experienced the importance of self-reflection.

The day before Jesus was arrested He celebrated what was, apparently, one of His favorite rituals of the Jewish faith: Passover. As a rabbi, it was His job to officiate the celebration. He did so with diligence, until He altered the rituals with a few remarkable deviations. The Lord Jesus forever changed the meaning of bread and wine when He called it His body and His blood. As many Christians now refer to it, the Lord's Supper is the ultimate example of what it means to pour your life out for others, but it's not on the ritual of Passover that I want to place our focus. It's on the other amazing selfless act Jesus performed that night where we will see the importance of self-reflection.

> *In order to live this life—His life—you must lose your own life.*

It was just before the Passover Festival. Jesus knew that the hour had come for him to leave this world and go to the Father. Having loved his own who were in the world, he loved them to the end.

The evening meal was in progress, and the devil had already prompted Judas, the son of Simon Iscariot, to betray Jesus. Jesus knew that the Father had put all things under his power, and that he had come from God and was returning to God; *so* he got up from the meal, took off his outer clothing, and wrapped a towel around his waist. After that, he poured water into a basin and began to wash his disciples' feet, drying them with the towel that was wrapped around him. (John 13:1-5 NIV, emphasis added)

Jesus Christ was both God and man as He walked the earth, and some of His largest miracles were seen in His restraint and the acts of humbleness He expressed in light of the fact that He was God. It appears in this account that the apostle John wanted to give us a glimpse into the mind and motivations of Jesus, whom he watched with such intense devotion.

It seems Jesus went through a time of self-evaluation before He became a servant to those men that night. You see in verse 3:

- Jesus reflected on His past—He knew where He had come from.

- He also evaluated His present—He understood the power He now possessed.

- And He knew and had complete confidence in His future—*so* He got up and served!

Just think of it. John shows us that Jesus's knowledge of His past, present, and ultimate future would be a powerful motivation and source of incredible strength; strength Jesus would need in the next several days as He endured the most horrendous torture and ultimate death—where He poured out His blood, power, forgiveness, peace, love, and life for all of us.

Jesus told us to deny ourselves, take up our cross, and follow Him (see Luke 9:23). What did He mean? Well, He did not tell us to take up our burdens, hold on to, study, look at, analyze, and talk about them for years—and then follow Him. The cross was not an instrument of burden. It was an instrument of death! Jesus said to die to yourself; crucify the deeds of the flesh and come and follow Him in order to live another life. In order to live this life—His life—you must lose your own life (see Matthew 16:25). We, as Christians, are citizens of an upside-down kingdom, not of this world, where the last shall be first, the greatest is the least, and in order to gain your life you must lose it.

All of this begins with a change of mind. It is not a one-time decision but a daily mind-set. Paul gave a life-changing instruction and insight into this process: "Let this mind be in you, which was also in Christ Jesus" (Philippians 2:5 KJV). You see, it is a "letting" process. You must let Him alter your thinking, motivations, and purpose. Let Him change the desires of your heart. Let Him into every aspect of your life. You must lose *your* mind in order to gain the mind of Christ. Because, until you change your mind, you will never change your behavior. This is the first step to living ANOTHER life.

NOTES

1. A. W. Tozer, *The Best of A. W. Tozer* (Camp Hill, PA: WingSpread, 2000), 203.

2. Bill Gillham, "Tuning In," Lifetime.org, May 1, 1996, www.lifetime.org/tuning-in-2/.

So What?

- Have you taken the time to look at your past to remember when you first met your Savior and how He began to change you? Describe your past briefly, in a cryptic response if you feel it is necessary.

- What do you think Jesus meant when He said He came that we might have an "abundant life" (see John 10:10)?

- How does this concept of an abundant life differ from what the world teaches?

Meditate on the following Scripture.

> Do nothing from selfish ambition or conceit, but in humility count others more significant than yourselves. Let each of you look not only to his own interests, but also to the interests of others. Have this mind among yourselves, which is yours in Christ Jesus, who, though he was in the form of God, did not count equality with God a thing to be grasped, but emptied himself, by taking the form of a servant, being born in the likeness of men. (Philippians 2:3-7)

In relation to the Scripture and what you have just read in chapter 1, list three ways Christ needs to alter your mindset to help you be more selfless.

I agree to allow Christ to alter _____.

I agree to allow Christ to alter _____.

I agree to allow Christ to alter _____.

- What are the two things that satisfied Jesus? Can you find satisfaction in those same two things in your life as well?

- What do you need to change in order to be satisfied in your life?

- Explain what it means to live a life as a funnel instead of a puddle. Would you say you are in "puddle mode" or "funnel mode" and how do you become a funnel?

- What are some examples of your "yucky flesh" and "good flesh"?

- What are some of the selfish "flesh issues" you have to die to daily as Paul taught?

- What are you presently using to fill the hole (lack of fulfillment) inside of you?

- After reading this chapter and reviewing these questions, what do you feel is God's purpose for your life?

- How can Jesus repurpose your life in accordance with His will? What will you need to change in order to fully follow His call?

- What is your one main takeaway from this chapter?

- Write a prayer of thanksgiving for your identity, your security, and the strength that Christ has given you.

Now What?

Go out and take a walk. Consider the abundant life God wants you to live. Look around as you walk and marvel in His great work. Give thanks for His forgiveness, grace, and all the ways He pours His love on you every day. Then begin to consider those whose lives you pour into. Ask God to bring to your mind someone you can begin to serve. Make plans to spend some time with that person and be open to how the Lord wants to use you as a funnel to pour His love through you to them.

Chapter Two

NOT TO US

The thief comes only to steal and kill and destroy. I came that
they may have life and have it abundantly.
John 10:10

The word *abundant* conjures visions of "overflowing."
It brings visions of a family's Thanksgiving table piled
high with platters of food, more than one family could begin
to consume. It is *more* than enough. Those who name Christ
as their Savior are promised an abundant life. God's intent is
to show the world His incredible grace, and He does this by
blessing His children and giving them more than they need.

There are many examples of this in Scripture: the woman
who filled jar after jar from the smallest container of oil in
the house (see 2 Kings 4:1-7), the story of Jesus multiplying
fishes and loaves (see Matthew 14:13-21; 15:32-38; Mark
6:30-44; 8:1-9; Luke 9:10-17; John 6:1-13), and God
providing manna from heaven (see Exodus 16:14) all show

that our God works in abundance and His children benefit from His blessings in awesome ways. Even light examination of these stories reveals this overarching theme: God's gifts to us are not merely for us but are to be shared. Yes, our needs are met in the process, but there is more to the giving of His gifts than that. The benefits of His blessings should not just stop with the blessed.

The Gifts God Gives His Children

Not to us, Lord, not to us but to your
name be the glory, because of your love and
faithfulness. (Psalm 115:1 NIV)

Our God is faithful and has lavished us with so much that it cannot be contained in one book. But that is just my point. His gifts to us should never be contained. They should spill out. They should flow through us to benefit those around us and glorify the name of God. They are not simply to and for us. These many blessings are tools given to us for the benefit of God's kingdom and to glorify its King.

PENTECOST
Not to Us

One of the very first gifts that God gave to humanity after Jesus's death was undoubtedly the most significant and life changing. It was the gift of the Holy Spirit.

When the day of Pentecost came, they were all together
in one place. Suddenly a sound like the blowing of a vi-
olent wind came from heaven and filled the whole house
where they were sitting. They saw what seemed to be
tongues of fire that separated and came to rest on each
of them. All of them were filled with the Holy Spirit and
began to speak in other tongues as the Spirit enabled
them. (Acts 2:1-4 NIV)

This was a pinnacle moment in history—when God
landed on each and every person in that room and poured
out His Spirit into each of them! And today we can have that
same Spirit poured into us. The Old Testament saints knew
that one day we would possess great power to overcome all
of life's obstacles, but they did not know how that power
would come about (see Ephesians 3:1-13). How could they
have known that God Himself would inhabit us in the person of the Holy Spirit?

Though this is a monumental day in the life of the
church, this is where many people stop in their study of Pentecost (with the incredible signs and wonders that occurred
on that day and the gifts that were given). But if we stop
there in the story, we miss the significance of this miraculous
event. Maybe we should ask the question, "Why did that
incredible miracle happen in the first place?"

Jesus gives part of the answer in Acts 1:8. He told His
disciples to stay in the city until power came upon them. In
Luke 24:13-25, we read that Jesus appeared to two of His
followers who were leaving Jerusalem, walking the road to

Emmaus, telling them to return. Why were they to stay in the city? We read in Luke 24:49: "I am going to send you what my Father has promised; but stay in the city until you have been clothed with power from on high" (NIV). He reiterated this promise of the Holy Spirit in Acts 1:8: "But you will receive power when the Holy Spirit has come upon you, and you will be my witnesses in Jerusalem and in all Judea and Samaria, and to the end of the earth."

Yes, the power of the Holy Spirit at Pentecost came, along with many signs and wonders. But it's clear from Acts 1:8 that one of the most amazing and meaningful purposes of the power poured out on them was the supernatural power needed for the purpose of *evangelism*. The same disciples who scattered to the wind at Christ's crucifixion now suddenly stood boldly with the Pentecostal power of the indwelling Holy Spirit, preaching to the thousands gathered: "Now there were dwelling in Jerusalem Jews, devout men from every nation under heaven. And at this sound the multitude came together, and they were bewildered, because each one was hearing them speak in his own language" (Acts 2:5-6).

Multitudes from different nations stood and heard the gospel preached in their native tongue. Yes, the disciples were filled with the gift of the Holy Spirit, but there was an immediate overflow. They began to pour out this "abundance" so that all nations might hear the saving power of Jesus Christ. Three thousand men and women were saved that day. That is abundance!

In my many travels I'm blown away by and, if I'm honest, sometimes a little envious of the incredible gifts God gives His children. Musicians, scientists, athletes, and brilliant business-minded people always amaze me. But I'm never surer of God's grace than when I meet pastors, missionaries, and lay-workers who clearly have a passion and talent for their work. When I encounter one of these gifted men and women, I immediately think, *How can this person be such a great evangelist/teacher/pastor?* Many of these servants are shy, soft-spoken, even socially awkward people who, in any normal setting, would be overlooked if you were looking for a "leader."

But then I have the privilege to work alongside these remarkable people and watch as God empowers them to do a work far outside their comfort zone, and I see incredible results for the kingdom of God. These men and women act, speak, and minister with a boldness, authority, and love that can only be attributed to a special anointing. Through their weakness He is made strong. And just as with the twelve simple men Jesus chose,

> *The flesh gratifies and glorifies self. The fruit of the Spirit magnifies selflessness and brings glory to God.*

God gets all the glory. People can see that in the flesh these servants could do very little, and it gives us all hope that God can even use us.

People may ask if the power of Pentecost is available today. I say yes! As long as evangelism and ministry are necessary on the planet, God's Pentecostal power will pour out in abundance. So Pentecost was not to us, but to His name.

THE FRUIT OF THE SPIRIT
Not to Us

But the fruit of the Spirit is love, joy, peace,
patience, kindness, goodness, faithfulness,
gentleness, self-control. (Galatians 5:22-23)

As we see, the first pouring out of the Spirit of God on men was not merely for them. So it follows that the fruit of that same Spirit is not just for us either. In his letter to the Galatians, Paul painted a picture of a life that is full of the fruit of the Spirit that came down at Pentecost. What a beautiful existence to live a life that expresses all those characteristics. On the surface, this list in Galatians depicts a life of fulfillment for the recipient. But before Paul lays out the benefits of the Spirit-led life, he warns us of the consequences of a life outside the direction of the Holy Spirit.

In Galatians 5:16, Paul says, "Walk by the *Spirit*, and you will not gratify the desires of the *flesh*" (emphasis added). He goes on to explain that our fleshly desires are contrary to the spirit. Paul then, in verses 19-21, proceeds to offer a list of the acts of the flesh such as sexual immorality, jealousy, and selfish ambition. All of these are *self*-gratifying, *self*-centered, and *selfish* sins. This "inventory of the flesh" exposes the contrast between walking "according to the flesh" or "according to the Spirit" (Romans 8:4 NKJV). The flesh gratifies and glorifies self. The fruit of the Spirit magnifies selflessness and brings glory to God.

On a side note, many have taught about the fruit of the Spirit. However, Paul teaches that it is one fruit composed of many aspects. It is no small distortion of the truth to teach otherwise. Paul taught us that when we walk in the Spirit, all of these traits will be expressed in us. And the opposite is also true. Someone who walks after the desires of the flesh will demonstrate all of the selfish, self-gratifying, and self-glorifying attitudes of his or her inventory of the flesh.

Let's take a look at a few aspects of the fruit of the Spirit and see that they are given for the benefit of others as well as the Spirit-filled Christian:

Love (is nothing if not given). Love produces very little if it is not expressed to others. The whole point of love is to build relationship, to care for someone else, to put others before yourself. How many popular songs throughout the years are focused on this one gift of God—that we can love each other? (This will age me, but my thoughts just went to every song ever written by Lionel Richie, Crosby, Stills & Nash, and yes, even Air Supply.)

Peace (is desired by everyone). Didn't Jesus say the *peacemakers* would be the sons of God (see Matthew 5:9)? Peacemakers do more than simply solve conflicts. These people exude peace. They make you feel better being in their presence. I think this is the case because as Jesus said in John 14:27, "Peace I leave with you; my peace I give to you. Not as the world gives do I give to you." We are intended to be the dispenser of peace, because the world cannot give this kind of peace.

Joy (is intended to be shared). Many summers I have had the privilege of traveling with and mentoring young men who serve our ministry as interns. At the end of the summer, I experience a bittersweet feeling as I send them out to complete their own ministry journey. Several of these men have gone on to lead incredible ministries. Knowing this, I have developed a time of commissioning, encouragement, and celebration as they begin their new calling. One of the elements of this tradition that has proved very meaningful is foot washing. As I wash my interns' feet, I will speak words of encouragement, of warning, and of final instructions.

As I talk to them, I am always drawn back to Romans 10:15: "How beautiful are the feet of those who preach the good news!" I explain to them that this statement was actually an old saying of that time, even before it became the written Word. It was a challenge to make sure there was always a "bounce in your step" when you entered a room; a challenge for individuals to carry themselves in such a way that they were perceived to always bring good news. It was an exhortation that we should bring joy with us wherever we go.

Being a joyful person is a magnetic quality that for many people will break down barriers. People, when they see you, should think, *The party starts now that he's here!* With this reputation, people will be much more likely to grant you permission to speak into their lives.

So, looking at the rest of the list of the fruit of the Spirit, we can see that patience, kindness, goodness, faithfulness, gentleness, and self-control are all relationship based. All are attitudes of the heart. They are depictions of a people person who considers others above himself or herself. These attributes were all given to us to use on *another*!

It needs to be said here that this fruit is produced naturally. Like breath, we only expel what is put in us. We breathe in the things of God and expel the things of God. The old saying goes, "Trees don't grunt to grow!" I am certain you've never seen a tree grunt to pass an apple! The roots go deep and the fruit comes out naturally. A plastic fruit factory is loud and hectic and smells bad. But a vineyard is quiet and peaceful. When we try to produce our own "plastic" fruit, we become louder, more hectic, and sooner or later our lives stink.

THE GIFTS OF THE SPIRIT
Not to Us

Now about the gifts of the Spirit, brothers and sisters, I do not want you to be uninformed. You know that when you were pagans, somehow or other you were influenced and led astray to mute idols. There-

39

*fore I want you to know that no one who
is speaking by the Spirit of God says, "Jesus
be cursed," and no one can say, "Jesus is
Lord," except by the Holy Spirit.*

*There are different kinds of gifts, but the
same Spirit distributes them. There are different kinds of service, but the same Lord.
There are different kinds of working, but
in all of them and in everyone it is the same
God at work.*

*Now to each one the manifestation of the
Spirit is given for the common good. To one
there is given through the Spirit a message
of wisdom, to another a message of knowledge by means of the same Spirit, to another faith by the same Spirit, to another gifts
of healing by that one Spirit, to another
miraculous powers, to another prophecy,
to another distinguishing between spirits,
to another speaking in different kinds of
tongues, and to still another the interpre-
tation of tongues. All these are the work of
one and the same Spirit, and he distributes
them to each one, just as he determines.
(1 Corinthians 12:1-11 NIV)*

There are many teachings on the gifts of the Spirit. Certain denominations focus on particular gifts. It is not the

purpose of this book to form a definitive list or doctrinal teaching on the gifts. Rather, what is apparent is that just like the fruit, the gifts of the Spirit are intended primarily as a ministry to others (see 1 Peter 4:10).

People who debate the validity of certain gifts usually cite flagrant abuses of the gifts to make their argument. But any investigation of the modern church will show a rampant abuse of almost all of the gifts of the Spirit in one way or another. The gift of teaching can be abused when people insert their own unbiblical opinions. The gift of knowledge is abused when unscriptural counseling practices are utilized. People are pretty creative when it comes to distorting the good things of God. But God gives these miraculous tools for the healing and uplifting of others. It is only when we take the reins and control from God and set off on our own course that true damage is done to the body of Christ.

First, we need a quick vocabulary lesson. I consider myself a wordsmith, not because I am great with words, but because I love to work with them. In fact, people have been known to laugh at my Bible when they see it because it's stuffed full of Post-it Notes. Each one has on it a word or phrase I don't understand. I am led through the Word not by my answers, but by my questions. When I run across words I don't know, I enjoy digging deeper into their meaning.

There are three words I want to define that will help us understand God's intended purpose of selflessness in those who receive gifts of the Spirit: *exalt*, *glorify*, and the seemingly insignificant word *of*.

Exalt. As a young, immature Christian at the age of twenty-two, I heard words and phrases during worship that confused me: "Here I raise mine Ebenezer." Mine what? I did not know why Jesus was the Lily of the Valley, and I never could point to which one was the Bright and Morning Star. I really did not know why the sweet old lady next to me wanted someone to "breathe on me."

My favorite worship chorus was "I Exalt Thee." My love for this old standard began when an old man in my church leaned over to me during that song one Sunday and whispered in my ear, "Do you know what *exalt* means? It means to lift Him up and make Him big!" I've never forgotten that moment. Up to that point in my life, everything was done to lift *me* up and make *me* big! Conviction overtook me at that moment and I repented of my selfishness right there…because of a definition!

Jesus found that word useful too. In the middle of one of His more harsh indictments of the teachers of His day, He said, "For those who *exalt* themselves will be humbled, and those who humble themselves will be *exalted*" (Matthew 23:12 NIV, emphasis added). The teachers of the law and Pharisees were experts at exalting themselves. It was expressed in the way they dressed as well as in their actions. In speaking of these men with the gift of teaching, Jesus said, "Everything they do is done for people to see" (Matthew 23:5 NIV). These men put on their fancy clothes and said their loud prayers in the public square so people would notice them and think they were so wise and holy.

But Jesus had no use for this display. It was the heart He was concerned about, and a heart that longed for Him did not do things for show. In the same way, many today exalt themselves with the gifts that God has given them.

Glorify. Another of my favorite old choruses is "Glorify Thy Name." In Scripture, the phrase "the glory of God" and the phrase "the presence of God" are virtually synonymous. The glory of God was in the pillar of fire that led Israel out of Egypt. The presence of God was in that pillar. The glory of God was in the burning bush that spoke with Moses, and the presence of God was in that burning bush. John 1:14 says, "The Word became flesh and made his dwelling among us. We have seen his glory, the glory of the one and only Son, who came from the Father, full of grace and truth" (NIV). Jesus was God in flesh, the presence of God walking on the planet. To glorify God, we are acknowledging His presence. When we say "We give You glory, God!" we are not giving God something He lost. We are acknowledging His presence in and through everything. Because He did all the work, He gets all the credit.

Of. This tiny connector word is often overlooked in the English language. Yet it has twenty-two different meanings as a preposition in the *Merriam-Webster* online dictionary, not to mention entries as a verb and an abbreviation.

Here's one example of the powerful use of that tiny word. Moses was standing out in a field one day after escaping Pharaoh's household. He was stripped of his title and most of his worldly possessions. He stood destitute by most standards of the world until God spoke to him and asked a curious question, "'What is that in your hand?' 'A staff,' he replied" (Exodus 4:2 NIV). I think everyone would agree that God knew what was in Moses' hand. I believe He asked Moses so Moses would *own* this stick and declare it as "his" staff.

Then God had Moses lay the staff down before Him. Now, the staff of a shepherd was a precious thing and most likely one of Moses' most valuable possessions. It was traditionally carved with the names of the shepherd's forefathers and was usually passed down to an heir. However, God wanted this staff, so Moses laid it down. Immediately the staff became a snake, and then God asked Moses to pick up the snake by the tail! This was quite a request. God first asked Moses to give up this precious possession and then He wanted Moses to take a step of faith by picking up the deadly serpent. Moses obeyed, and instantly the staff reappeared in the place of the snake in his hand.

On the surface this seems like an insignificant miracle, but something changed in the staff that day. This same staff became the one Moses held up to empower the Israelites to win a battle. This same staff was used by Moses to strike a rock in the desert and bring forth water. The same staff was used by Moses to split the Red Sea!

What happened? Why did such an inanimate object now carry so much power? *Because it changed ownership that day!* Exodus 17:9 says, "Moses said to Joshua, 'Choose some of our men and go out to fight the Amalekites. Tomorrow I will stand on top of the hill with *the staff of God* in my hands'"

(NIV, emphasis added). Moses' staff became the staff *of* God. Do you see it? He now held the staff *of* God in his hands!

What had been a simple stick now held incredible power because the day Moses laid it down and gave it to God, it *changed ownership*. One of those definitions from *Webster's Dictionary* says the word *of* is "used as a function word to indicate belonging or a possessive relationship." Because the staff now belonged to God, it could wield power only when it was operated and used by God for His will and His glory. In the same way, the gifts of the Spirit and fruit of the Spirit, as well as the children of God, will only possess power when they are owned, operated, and used to *exalt* and *glorify* God.

> *Glorify the* LORD *with me; let us exalt his name together. (Psalm 34:3 NIV)*

THE CHURCH
Not to Us

The most apparent expressions of selfishness in the church happen when members consider the church "their" church; the ones who say, "That's my pew," or "He's my pastor," or "Look at those stained glass windows my money bought." Ownership is useful only if it's used to express a member's responsibility to grow and nurture people and to reach out to the community, and it can destroy a fellowship if it's misused because of pride. Though there is nothing wrong with honoring past members and loved ones, there are churches built on thousands of plaques and spaces in the church dedicated to everyone...but Christ. I have actually stood in a pulpit only to discover that the very microphone *cable* I was speaking through had a plaque dangling from it in honor of someone! But that is not the most troubling trend we see in Christians today.

Recently, in the blog of a fellow Christian author, I read of his decision to step away from corporate worship. He was not recommending that for everyone, but he decided he no longer needed the "organized" church. People are all wired differently, and some may not respond to a particular kind of music or expressions of corporate worship the same as others do, but our church attendance was never intended for us to simply receive blessings. Yet this emerging thought has cropped up many times in conversations with others in the last few years. This is a cause for concern because the need for the local body is as important today as ever.

There comes a season in the life of a mature Christian where Sunday-morning sermons may not meet the needs of where they are spiritually. It may be that a certain type of worship is not appealing. Even the need for community may be met in other ways in their lives. But it occurs to me that most of these excuses not to be involved in a church community are based on a "consumerist" attitude toward church.

When a Christian decides that the church is not meeting his or her needs, that Christian should first focus on *serving* the church!

Now, let me be clear, if a pastor's teaching is not consistently biblically sound, that may be a reason for you to separate from that congregation. But it is important to remember that just because the pastor's message this Sunday didn't speak to you and where you are in your journey with Christ doesn't mean it wasn't exactly what the person sitting next to you needed to hear.

God said, "My glory I will not give to another." You and I are "another" too.

Instead of neglecting the words of Paul when he said, "Let us consider how we may spur one another on toward love and good deeds, not giving up meeting together, as some are in the habit of doing, but encouraging one another—and all the more as you see the Day approaching" (Hebrews 10:24-25 NIV), a mature Christian should come to church with open eyes and with a heart willing to serve younger Christians. They are sitting all around you! You should attend with the selfless purpose of helping them to "rightly divide the Word of God" and should emulate qualities of a fully devoted follower of Christ (2 Timothy 2:15). Many "seasoned" Christians fall into the trap of becoming mere spectators in worship, acting as critics of sermons, song choices, lighting, sound, and even the church decor! Jesus would refer to these folks as "whitewashed tombs" (Matthew 23:27). On the outside they look beautiful, and perhaps even holy, but inside they are lifeless.

As a "baby Christian," I was aware that the old man sitting next to me in church, the one I mentioned who taught me about exalting the Lord, probably didn't learn anything new from elementary teachings out of the Word of God. But he knew he was there to encourage me and to be a model. He probably also understood that the Word of God never comes back void and that each time it is preached, a Christian can gain some knowledge or receive some encouragement.

I grew through "holy envy," looking at the men and women who were so much further along in their walk with Christ than I was. I still do. I wanted the abundant life that was so apparent in them. I truly appreciated these "subtle mentors," who chose to pour their lives into me through the years. They gently corrected and molded me when I needed it and enjoyed my many questions and energy as I grew.

We mature Christians need to do the same to the next generation of believers in the local church. So the next time you are in the pew and are focused on what you are not getting out of the message, find a way to live out that message to those around you. They could be watching you right then.

❦❦❦

Pentecost, the church, and all of the gifts, fruits, and blessings of God are never intended merely for man or to glorify anyone but God Himself. In Isaiah 14:12-14, Satan said that he desired to exalt himself. He wanted all the glory. Yet in Isaiah 48:11, God said, "My glory I will not give to another." You and I are "another" too. It should be exciting to know that God intends to give so much to us,

His children. One of the most comforting things is that He would choose us at all. Some of us feel so unworthy to receive this abundance. But then again, Christianity is best suited for the weakest vessels because in your weakness He is made strong (see 2 Corinthians 12:9). He likes to use the weakest vessels to pour His abundance through because if He is to get all the glory, then it must be apparent that He did all the work. I know I'm glad that God chooses the weak things of this world.

Again, we weak vessels say in a loud voice, "Not to us, O LORD, not to us, but to your name give glory" (Psalm 115:1).

So What?

Meditate on the following Scripture.

> But the fruit of the Spirit is love, joy, peace, patience, kindness, goodness, faithfulness, gentleness, self-control; against such things there is no law. And those who belong to Christ Jesus have crucified the flesh with its passions and desires. If we live by the Spirit, let us keep in step with the Spirit. (Galatians 5:22-25)

- Reflect on the blessings God has given you. List the top five gifts, talents, or blessings you believe the Lord has blessed you with.

Of the five gifts you have listed above, how many are spiritual gifts? There is no shame or guilt if you listed family members or worldly items. But take a few more minutes to consider the spiritual gifts you have been given. Look back over the list and add to it those spiritual gifts you have received.

- Read Acts 1–2. List one of the purposes for the pouring out of the Holy Spirit.

- Define *evangelism*.

- How is the Holy Spirit involved in evangelism?

- In the same manner, how can the Holy Spirit work through you for the purpose of evangelism?

Give an antonym to each fruit of the Spirit (an example is provided).

ex. Love: Hate

Joy:

Peace:

Patience:

Longsuffering:

Kindness:

Goodness:

Faithfulness:

Gentleness:

Self-control:

- Be honest with yourself: which fruit of the Spirit do you struggle with the most?

- Write down the top three areas you are led to work on and how you can begin to make those changes.

- Read 1 Corinthians 12:1-11 and list the gifts of the Spirit in the passage here.

- Give examples of how the gifts are used for God's purposes and how the gifts can also be abused for man's own purposes.

- Which of these gifts do you feel you've been given?

- Do you feel you are using these gifts to their fullest potential for the kingdom? If not, what behavior or attitude can help you make this adjustment?

Thinking on the fruit and the gifts of the Spirit that God has given you, have you truly laid them before the Lord as Moses did? Stop and ask God to take and use those gifts (and you) as He sees fit for His glory.

Complete the following sentence: When a Christian decides that the church is not meeting his or her needs, that Christian should first focus on _____.

- How do you believe you can better use the gifts, talents, and fruits God has given you to advance the kingdom of God through His church?

- What is your one main takeaway from this chapter?

Now What?

Reflect on the people in your life who have been spiritual mentors to you. Did they mentor you by instruction or simply by the way they lived their lives? Have you ever told them how they affected your life by pouring into you?

During this week, contact those people and show your appreciation for their spiritual walk. Then make a phone call to your church and ask how you can begin to better pour out through your local body of believers.

Chapter Three

WOUNDS THAT HEAL

He himself bore our sins in his body on the tree, that we might die to sin and live to righteousness. By his wounds you have been healed.

1 Peter 2:24

One evening as I was studying in my office, the phone rang. I spoke with a young woman I had taught in a Bible study some years before. I had counseled and guided her during her college years as she dealt with self-esteem issues and other normal challenges of college life. She was calling because she had hit a rough patch and thought she needed to go deeper into the issues of her past. She thought she and I could dig up all the suppressed dysfunctions that she *just knew* must still be hidden in her psyche. These were, in her words, "obviously causing all my present-day social anxieties and problems."

This discussion led me to employ a quirky, unorthodox

response inspired again by Michael Wells. I explained that I, too, believed her counseling needs were much bigger than we first imagined. In fact, I expressed to her that she probably needed dozens of hours of counseling. Unfortunately, that would be very expensive. I would have to charge her at least $70 an hour (which was not true in the least).

But I said I had a deal for her. I would reduce her rate if she would drive north of Nashville and find a beautiful, sprawling farm. Then I wanted her to go to a lovely pasture and locate a nice cow patty. Once she found it, she was to sit with it for several hours a day, and she was to study, dissect, and explore this cow patty. I explained that she should really "get in there" and feel it, smell it, squish it between her fingers…anything she could do to really explore the "complexity" of that cow poo!

After her initial reaction of shock, I asked her, "At the end of dozens of hours of studying this cow patty, what will you know?"

"Nothing!" she said. "It's just a cow patty!"

"Good answer!" I responded. "You will know nothing more about the cow patty than when you first sat down except that you will now smell like it!"

I shared with her that when I was growing up, my grandfather had a farm and I often played in the fields. It only took one experience of running barefoot in the pasture to understand, with complete clarity, the essence of a patty. I learned that first day what to do with a cow patty: step around it or let it dry up and kick it out of the way.

Yes, we could dig further into her past...again. But after years of digging and uncovering all the dirt she could find, it would still be *just dirt*! Then I explained a life-altering truth I've learned that

> *A person of wisdom is the sum of all the positives and the negatives in life.*

guides me to this day: *what gets your attention gets you*! If she just focused on the "dirt" in her past, she could relive it, mourn it, and dissect it, but it might not accomplish much except to make her wallow in it until she smelled like it. Yes, it was good to embrace her wounded past and examine her life, but sooner than later, she must strive to move past it and focus on Christ and *His* life. Then true healing would begin.

Many people will say that time heals all wounds. I'm not sure that this is completely true. Memories from wounds and pain from loss, abuse, and injustices are not always erased by time. Healing does not mean "holy amnesia."

Walking with Wounds

In the immediate aftermath of a tragic event in our lives, pain "walks on top of us," oppressing us, controlling our moods and our motivations. It clouds our thinking and affects every relationship.

These painful times can paralyze us for a season. When a painful experience initially happens, we might be in a state of shock. At this point, the best prescription for health could be a period of rest and inactivity. Sometimes we will feel the need to withdraw from others and take time to rest in order for emotions to return to reality. Over time, however, as healing begins, that pain will begin to "walk beside us." Pain will become our "invisible friend."

As toddlers, many of us had invisible friends, that friend who was always there for us. They comforted us and appeared when we needed them most. That friend was also who we blamed when things went wrong. ("My friend Johnny messed up my room, Mom, not me!")

In the same way, pain begins to walk beside us as an invisible friend. Pain becomes the thing we hold on to whenever we need a crutch. We can also make our "painful" friend appear when we want something to blame for the mood we are in or we want an excuse for any bad behavior or choices we might make. These behaviors, if left unchecked, can result in a period of lost friendships and a time when loved ones become victims of our wounds.

Many people, tragically, never truly walk out of this stage and instead remain, in their minds, victims for the rest of their lives. Their identities are anchored in their past, their pain, and their wounds. They become the walking wounded. Others, over time, begin to understand the grace, forgiveness, and second chances offered by Jesus Christ. They start to pray again. They reach out to others. They learn to forgive the one whom they believe is responsible for the pain or they begin to accept that, though they may not understand His ways, God is always in control and His plans are ultimately good. This is when they move from being victims to being victorious over their pain. They begin to see that what Satan meant for evil, God can use for good. They experience God in new ways as He gives them beauty for ashes and strength for fear (see Isaiah 61:3). The joy of knowing Jesus Christ is this: we never need to remain victims in Christ Jesus.

We can, through prayer, the power of forgiveness, the love and comfort of others, and the healing that only God can bring begin to "walk on top of the pain." The pain is still there. The pain still stings like a stone in our shoe, but we can control it now. There are times we may want to lie down and wallow in the pain, but for the most part, it stays at our feet. This is when a beautiful thing happens: the pain begins to absorb into us as we walk on top of it. It never completely disappears nor should we want it to. The pain becomes a part of us. The wound becomes a part of our wisdom. A person of wisdom is the sum of all the positives *and* the negatives in life. Pain is no longer a dragon bent on destroying us. It lives only as an annoying little gnat, constantly reminding us that life is real and that every day is not full of butterflies. But we can flick it away and begin to see that the butterflies will come out again.

It's only then that we may see true miracles in our lives. And for the rest of our lives, we can walk, used by God, as wounded healers in the lives of others.

The Wounded Healer

Not long ago, I was at a large conference and saw God moving in amazing ways in the lives of hundreds of people. At the end of the service I was standing by the stage talking with people when a twenty-five-year-old woman, who seemed very timid but full of joy, approached me. She thanked me for being very real with the audience, and I appreciated her encouragement. Then she asked a question I have never been asked before, and it both shocked me and solidified my philosophy of healing. Sheepishly she asked, "Is it OK for me to thank God for the sexual abuse in my past?"

I had to process this question for just a moment before I answered her. I prayed and asked God to give me discernment as to how I should respond. I said, "First, tell me what you mean and then I will tell you if it's a good thing."

She went on to explain that though her abuse had been a tragedy in her life, she had sought out great Christian counseling. She had been through an incredible healing process. She was thanking God because she believed that He had taken everything that Satan meant for evil in her life and used it for good. She said she believed she became a sensitive and discerning person who saw pain in the eyes of other abused girls and was able to give them hope and healing *because* of her own wounds. She had become the definition of a wounded healer!

I said, "My friend, if that is not healing, I don't know

what is!" God had not only healed her, but was beginning to pour healing out of the very wounds of her heart.

When I was in elementary school, I was a firebug. In fact, I got the worst spanking of my life because I almost burned down our house. (That's a story for another book.) My best friend and I were always partners in crime. We shot things (and other people) with BB guns, got in mud fights, put lizards in my sister's shoes, and did all the mischievous things that little rug rats do. Our favorite activity was sneaking away to experiment with—you guessed it—fire. Because of my little "hobby," I can tell you what color flame each type of fuel makes and which types of plastic make the best fires or melt the quickest.

One day, as my friend and I were involved in one of our pyromaniac adventures, we discovered that burning a milk jug makes a stream of hot plastic that resembles bullets and makes a sound like bombs coming out of airplanes! (At least the ones we saw in the movies.) We immediately decided that we should go and attack the fire ant mounds in the backyard. As I went in for a "dive bomb" run to destroy those evil fire ants, my friend decided to do the same and accidentally poured hot, burning plastic on my finger. This episode resulted in various antibiotics, Band-Aids, and the familiar grounding from my parents.

But that wasn't all: to this day I can still see the damage done by that one painful act. I carry a scar. A scar is created when the body heals from an injury. As a matter of fact, I cannot wear a ring on my right ring finger because there is a bump there that becomes very irritated. Often there is "too much healing" that results in an excess of skin. Doctors often use what is called dermabrasion to remove the excess skin from a scar. In the same way, when God heals us from the many emotional and tragic events (scars) of our lives, He heals us "too much." The result is that we can pour out this excess healing to others.

You see, God pours His power through the very wounds of our lives. This is why some of the best counselors for issues such as alcoholism and abuse are people who have been healed from abuse or alcoholism. Put simply, the final, constant, and evolving state of healing is when we begin to pour out healing to others. Peter, quoting Isaiah, told us, "By [Jesus's] wounds you have been healed" (1 Peter 2:24). In the same way, by *your* wounds, you can heal others when you "scrape off" the excess healing and pour out the wisdom and knowledge you give to others.

The Healing Found in "Another"

When we pour out healing to others, it does not mean we are immune from painful experiences in our own lives. God will continue to work His healing in us even as we serve others. As we walk with others and experience life together, things can get messy. Relationships can be a source of pain and wounding, especially when people are being vulnerable and letting their true selves and struggles out. Relationships can also be a major vehicle God uses to bring about continued growth and healing.

In our ministry I've talked to many singles. Some believe that if they just get married, the "magic ring" will fix all of their problems and heal all their wounds. But once they have found a match, the couple soon realizes that marriage brings to the surface many wounds and issues of each individual rather than cures them. Relationships often reveal insecurities, anger, and dysfunctional thought processes. All relationships have the ability to bring up all of our deep flaws and issues. During these times we need to understand and hold on to this truth:

Anything God reveals, He intends to heal.

One of the joys of my life as a Christian communicator is the simple truth that "the heavens declare the glory of God" (Psalm 19:1). To me that means everything preaches Jesus, if you just look at it long enough. God's truths can be found in all of nature. And, as much as some would deny it, God is written into everything that we do and everything we are.

One example of how God writes Himself into everything we see and do is found in Malachi 3. The prophet states that our God sits as a refiner and purifier of gold and silver (see v. 3). What does God purify like gold and silver? He purifies us. God speaks to the prophet Jeremiah and tells him that he is to be "a tester of metals" and that His people are the ore (Jeremiah 6:27). God was referring to the refining process of gold and silver in both of these references. Let's take a closer look at the refining process to see what God is saying to us.

The process people have used to refine gold and silver has not changed much in several thousand years. Precious metals come out of the ground in the form of ore and must first be refined by fire before they can be used. The ore is heated to a liquid state. As the ore is superheated, all of its impurities float to the surface as dross or slag. The next part of the process is to scrape off the dross or slag. Afterward, the smith will add an alkali. This is a base substance that causes more impurities to rise to the surface in order to be removed.

At that point the gold or silver will look pure to the naked eye, *but it is not*. The final stage of refining requires lead to be added to the liquid mix. The lead acts as a magnet and draws all trace metals to it. These metals and impurities cannot be seen but still defile the purity of the precious metal. When the process has been repeated multiple times, the smith can declare whether the gold or silver in front of him or her is pure.

This is an amazing description of God's transformation process in a Christian. Just like in the refining process of gold and silver, God allows things to "heat up" in our friendships, our jobs, our families, our health, our children so that all of the "trash" will boil to the surface. Then God scrapes those things off of our lives.

God will bring different people in your life to aid in this purifying process. There will be times in your life when you will find yourself in the company of people who bring out the worst in you. One person might bring out insecurities. Another will bring up lust, greed, anger, or self-control issues. God orchestrated and allowed these people into your life to bring out these hidden impurities. These impurities may not be apparent to the naked eye when looking at your life, but they are there, buried deep within your flesh. These people draw issues out like a magnet. They are the "lead" that God has added to your life. When God reveals these issues and boils them up, you are to scrape them off and *get the lead out*. God allows the situations of our lives to strip us of all that is not of Him.

And just a warning: this is not something that is one and done. This process will occur more than once over your lifetime because we often need "remedial school" in certain areas of our lives. God goes deeper and deeper, revealing hidden issues at different stages of your walk with Him. He continues this healing throughout our lives, but we won't be fully healed until we reach heaven.

Tips and Words of Warning to Wounded Healers

The awesome privilege and frightening responsibility of leading people in a time of "invitation" at conferences and churches is a task I take very seriously. The joy of seeing hearts surrender to Christ and His will is overwhelming, and I will never get used to it. It is even more sobering to know that some of these people will eventually step into the roles of mentor, disciple maker, counselor, or healer, and some will even likely go on to become full-time vocational ministers. So I always feel the need to pour some initial wisdom into them while I can.

One day a young man stood straight up with tears in his eyes when I asked if there was anyone present who felt God's call to full-time vocational service. He then joined the others who felt the same in a small room behind the sanctuary. They waited for me and their own pastors to come for a time of prayer. I entered the room full of these young, resolute, future leaders and began by telling them this piece of advice: "Don't do it! Run! There will be pain and disappointment and sacrifice!" There was complete silence until I let a smirk slip onto my face. Then the room erupted in the laughter and joy that I believe should inaugurate anyone into the service of the gospel.

But the truth is that everything I said was accurate (except the "don't do it" part). Those who are called to invest in others will not always see a return on their investment, and many will experience times of discouragement when they give of themselves for the sake of another's growth. That is because we are dealing with flesh and blood and personalities and habits and sin. We wage war against motivations, dysfunction, prejudice, ignorance, and all the ridiculousness that is part of being human. It's comforting to know that even Jesus seemed to be frustrated at dealing with people to the point of declaring, "How long shall I put up with you?" (Matthew 17:17 NIV).

We can also learn much from how Jesus dealt with those He healed and counseled. One day, He delivered a hard message to a rich young man about the cost of following Him, and the young man outright rejected His counsel (Mark 10). He had to react with love and patience with His disciples (including Judas), whom He knew would deny and betray Him. And He had to constantly respond to the doubt, fear, and rebellion of those He was to die for. But He poured out grace and understanding to all of them. Just as Jesus always responded with understanding, patience, and healing, we as wounded healers need to be instruments of those attributes when dealing with others.

One incident where we can learn the way Jesus dealt with those in need of healing is His encounter with the invalid man at the pool of Bethesda in John 5.

> Some time later, Jesus went up to Jerusalem for one of the Jewish festivals. Now there is in Jerusalem near the Sheep Gate a pool, which in Aramaic is called Bethesda and which is surrounded by five covered colonnades. Here a great number of disabled people used to lie—the blind, the lame, and the paralyzed. One who was there had been an invalid for thirty-eight years. When Jesus saw him lying there and learned that he had been in this condition for a long time, he asked him, "Do you want to get well?"
>
> "Sir," the invalid replied, "I have no one to help me into the pool when the water is stirred. While I am trying to get in, someone else goes down ahead of me."

Then Jesus said to him, "Get up! Pick up your mat and walk." At once the man was cured; he picked up his mat and walked.

The day on which this took place was a Sabbath.
(John 5:1-9 NIV)

As Jesus was standing before this man who had been an invalid for thirty-eight years, I'm sure His followers were ready to celebrate this miracle like so many they had seen before. I think they were wondering, *Is He going to spit in the mud or speak loudly to the spirit that is oppressing the crippled man?* So I think it would have been a bit surprising when Jesus simply asked the man a strange question that seemed to have an obvious answer: "Do you want to get well?" So why did He ask?

Exploring His motives for this question will help us better deal with hurting people. Here are a few bits of wisdom we can glean from this encounter.

1. *Be a hope giver.* Some Bible teachers believe Jesus asked this to give this man's heart hope. Hope is a powerful force in the process of healing. We need to constantly remind others of the fact that there is a light at the end of the tunnel, and that with Christ the Light will come to them!

In the horrific Porsolt swim tests of the 1950s, rats were placed in acrylic cylinders filled with water and forced to swim. One group experienced the "hope" of rescue and the others did not. Inevitably, the "hope group" survived days longer than the "no hope group."

This gruesome test reflects a truth: we need hope to survive. Paul reminds us of this in Romans: "We know that suffering produces perseverance; perseverance, character; and character, hope. And hope does not put us to shame" (Romans 5:3-5 NIV). When we encounter people who feel they are drowning in the midst of life's struggles, we are to remind them that we have a God who has not left us but dives into our deepest moments and pulls us out. He doesn't just hold us up and keep our heads above water; He draws us out of the sea and places us on dry land (see Psalm 18).

We should also encourage people to surround themselves with an atmosphere and people "of hope." When Jesus asked this man if he wanted healing, the man immediately responded by reminding Jesus that it was impossible to get to the healing waters of the Bethesda because he was crippled. How many years had he stayed there right beside a place that offered the hope of his healing but with no one who would help him get there? This is a question I ask many people when I'm counseling them. People should try to surround themselves with positive, forward-thinking people and avoid those who bring them down. The "no hope group" will never get them to the place of healing.

2. *Point them to the Healer.* Some believe Jesus's question was to get the man's eyes fixed on Him. At the very least, the question, "Do you want to get well?" would have been met with a sarcastic look from a crippled man who lay by a lake known for healing every day. "Really? Do I want to get well? No, I'm just tanning!"

71

Whatever his reaction, I believe that man would have been curious enough to turn his sore eyes from the constant vigil of staring at the pool for a ripple that was the sign that the "healing angel" was "troubling the waters" and look at Jesus. You see, he needed to turn and see where his healing was about to come from: Jesus. Though "Turn Your Eyes upon Jesus" is a beautiful old hymn, it is also a powerful truth.

Michael Wells coined the phrase "There is nothing the nearness of God won't fix!" That simply means if you focus on your problems, they will overcome you every time. But if you focus on Christ, your problems will fade. Draw near to Him and He will draw near to you (see James 4:8).

3. *Some hearts refuse to be comforted.* There are many theories about Jesus's motives for asking that peculiar question, but the simple and most profound truth may be this: Jesus wanted to know if the invalid wanted to be healed. Was he sure he wanted this miracle?

Understand that this man had lived for thirty-eight years dependent on others. People helped him dress, bathed him, and brought him food. Someone provided his shelter and transportation. If he were healed, he would have to get a job! He would have to provide for himself and maybe even help others! He would no longer have an excuse for his moodiness, laziness, or any times he had used his infirmity as a reason for selfish and sinful behavior.

> *Getting involved in the life of another is worth it.*

There will always be people you encounter who say they want to get better but really do not want the responsibility of a healthy, productive life. They prefer to remain victims, and so the old colloquialism rings true: you can lead a horse [or person] to water, but you cannot make him drink. The message of the gospel is for us to present the truth of salvation and healing to others. The ultimate decision of whether they will know the truth so the truth can set them free rests solely on them.

You Can't Fix Anyone

Though it seems obvious, the reality that we cannot fix *anyone* needs to be stated because our pride, heart, and compassion can often cloud this truth as we try to lift someone out of pain. We can get caught up in the satisfaction and self-importance that we feel while investing in others. In the process we serve these people poorly when we point them to ourselves instead of Christ. Also, we can get caught up by the "sin which so easily ensnares us" (Hebrews 12:1 NKJV) when we engulf ourselves in the problems and sins of others.

I had the privilege of knowing a wonderful surgeon named Dr. William Jernigan. Dr. Jernigan was a strong believer, and I often used him as a resource of wisdom. He was always free with his advice and wonderful stories. He once told me that our jobs (minister and surgeon) were a lot alike. I was very flattered but asked him to explain further. He went on to say that he had to learn early on in his career that he could not heal anyone. His job was to "patch up the broken stuff" and then create a healing atmosphere. Then he just sat back and watched God do the healing. Our job in the lives of the hurting and broken may be to protect, advise, comfort, educate, and create an atmosphere of healing, but only God can mend a soul.

I'd like to offer a caution here: sin is not just destructive to the person mired in it but can also damage those who want to lift someone out of his or her sin. The temptations, depression, and other issues of the counselee can easily suck in the counselor because of the vulnerability required in this kind of relationship. As Jesus warned us, some issues require "much prayer."

How do you keep from getting sucked in? Make sure there is always someone who holds you accountable in your spiritual life, especially if you are mentoring or assisting someone else. This person will help you remain close to the cross as you are helping others. Second, always make sure that you counsel from His wisdom, His Word, not your own. This will ensure that our egos and our flesh will not get in our own way or in the way of those we counsel.

Not Everyone You Reach Out to Will Be Healed

At Bethesda, Jesus was undoubtedly surrounded by many people in need of healing. It's important to note that we have no account of Him healing everyone else who came to Bethesda, "the place of healing," except for that one man. I don't believe that Jesus healed every person with sickness while He walked the earth, nor do I believe that He heals everyone who asks today. That does not mean I lack faith in Him. It means I have faith His will is best for me and for you.

We pray for someone to be healed, but how do we know what that healing will look like? What if the best thing for that person was to get sick? What if God is most glorified through that person's weakness? How do we really know what is evil and what is good? Yes, it is good to ask for healing with the faith that God can do anything, but we should always profess, as Jesus did in the garden of Gethsemane when He knew the time for the cross was drawing near, "Not my will, but yours be done" (Luke 22:42 NIV). We should count on the grace of God as Paul did when God said to him, "My grace is sufficient" (2 Corinthians 12:9).

Despite all the warnings and cautions I have given, I want to encourage you even more. Getting involved in the life of another is worth it. For all the pain and sacrifice, the knowledge that you are being the hands, feet, mouth, and ears of the body of Christ fulfills what I believe is the full ministry of the gospel of Jesus. And while that is our primary goal and charge, this service will bring about fulfillment for you as well.

At the beginning of this chapter, I spoke of the young lady and the cow patties. Though it meant a decades-long investment in her life, with me constantly telling her there was a light at the end of the tunnel, she has indeed come out of the tunnel and into the light and is now helping others.

The reward is worth all the struggles, fears, and doubts that come our way. Allowing Him to heal our wounds gives Him the power to use us to heal others as well.

So What?

Meditate on the following Scripture.

> He was despised and rejected by men,
>   a man of sorrows and acquainted with grief;
> and as one from whom men hide their faces
>   he was despised, and we esteemed him not.
>
> Surely he has borne our griefs
>   and carried our sorrows;
> yet we esteemed him stricken,
>   smitten by God, and afflicted.
> But he was pierced for our transgressions;
>   he was crushed for our iniquities;
> upon him was the chastisement that brought us peace,
>   and with his wounds we are healed.
>   Isaiah 53:3-5

- What wounds have you sustained in life? Are they physical? Are they spiritual? Take a few minutes and list them here.

- How long did you wallow in your own wounds? Did they fester like an untreated sore? Did they infect others around you? Briefly make notes to remind yourself:

- Reflect on a time when you were spiritually wounded. Did you attempt to heal yourself? Did you call out to the Great Physician for His healing power? How did He respond to your cries?

- Have you met anyone who has walked a similar path? If so, how was that person able to minister to you in your time of need? How were you able to minister to that person in turn?

- How did you come to embrace the healing of Christ and walk on top of the pain? Do you still need to overcome some of the deeper wounds?

If you are in the middle of a "healing time" right now, in what stage discussed in the chapter would you place yourself? Circle the sentence below that best describes your process now. Explain your choice.

The pain walks on top of me.

The pain walks beside me.

I walk on top of the pain.

The pain is absorbing into me and becoming part of the "healed me."

- In your own words, describe what it means to be a wounded healer.

- Finish this sentence: One of the final stages of healing is when we begin to _____ to others.

- Thinking back to the discussion of the refining fire, consider the description of how precious metals are purified. How has God brought positive people and circumstances into your life to aid in your purifying process? List some of those individuals and share how God used them for your betterment.

- What is a hope giver? How can you be one?

- How can you direct someone to the Healer?

- Some hearts refuse to be comforted. When this is the case, what can we do to help people during these instances?

- What are two things you can do to keep from being sucked in to another person's pit of despair?

- What is your one main takeaway from this chapter?

Now What?

Look around you and think of individuals who may be struggling with a pain similar to what you have experienced. Could they benefit from the excess healing that God has brought about from your wounds? Write their names down below.

As you look at each name, pray and ask God to use you, if it's His will, to be a wounded healer in that person's life. Reach out to that individual and offer to help, if at all possible.

If you are unable to think of a person, reach out to a local organization or support group to serve. You may be the hands and feet that the body of Christ needs to fulfill His gospel.

THE "ANOTHERS"

Chapter Four

"ANOTHER" CHAPTER (OR TWO)

*For you were called to freedom, brothers. Only do not use
your freedom as an opportunity for the flesh, but through
love serve one another.*
Galatians 5:13

There is a wonderful old story of a pastor who preached
the same sermon over and over. Finally, a parishioner
got up the nerve to ask him why. The pastor smiled and said
it was because the congregation came in every week looking like they had forgotten what he had preached the week
before.

We can never look at the foundational truths of being a
Christian and following Christ too much or dive into them
deep enough because they go to the heart of God, which is
a great mystery. So we should never assume that "we've got
this." We can never learn enough about God's Word and
what it means to serve Him and others.

For the next few chapters, we are going to look at some "anothers" in Scripture. We will explore topics that some would consider elementary teachings that have been repeatedly discussed for years. Topics such as loving one another, exhorting one another, and comforting one another are common themes in today's church sermons—and we can never look at them enough. We are never *finished* learning about God.

Thus, before we dive in, I submit to you that these actually are not elementary teachings. If these topics and teachings are so basic, why are so many Christians failing at them? Why are these fundamental truths at the core of so many problems in our families, countries, and the world? Are we like those parishioners who heard the same messages over and over but never really absorbed their meaning? How do we forget these lessons so quickly?

I believe Jesus knew our propensity to forget. In fact, I think that's one of the many reasons that He instituted the sacraments of baptism and communion. These are both physical acts we are to perform to help us remember all He has done for us. (Remember when He said, "Do this in remembrance of me"? [Luke 22:19].)

Paul also understood the importance of reiterating truths. He said we should continually return to the fundamental teachings of God (see Hebrews 5:12). Whether it is accidental, deliberate, or simply laziness in the case of the Hebrews Paul was speaking to, we need to occasionally stop and take inventory of our lives to see where we have walked away from the truth. So, let's look again at these lessons. I know that I, like many people, find myself in "spiritual remedial class" over and over. I am relearning the fundamentals of being a disciple as God brings me through circumstances. That is true of many of the deepest truths of God.

As I travel to many churches, often I am asked by pastors and student ministers to "go deep." I am told that their people need to be challenged with deeper truths. My response to them is always the same: there are no deeper truths than that God loves me for no good reason, and He forgives me completely and wants me to show that love to others. I will never get over God's amazing desire to redeem me, to make more of me than I could ever imagine, and that He intends to accomplish this, not by helping me with my little life but by actually living His life through me! I draw deeper and deeper into the well of those truths every year that I exist on this planet. So let's look at some of these deep, basic "anothers" of our faith.

Love One Another

"A new command I give you: Love one another. As I have loved you, so you must love one another." (John 13:34 NIV)

Rarely do I ever feel that I am loving others more than when I am traveling and ministering in the country of Haiti. Our ministry has been serving the Haitian people since 2002. So when the devastating earthquake rocked Haiti on

January 12, 2010, I am proud to say some from our ministry were among the first feet on the ground. In fact, we arrived in a private plane in the middle of the night when the airport was still damaged and closed. We were the first plane to arrive on the tarmac after the earthquake, and we slept alone on the concrete that first night while airport night guards watched over us. We did not go because we were an aid organization but because we were worried about our friends and those we loved. Anytime a natural disaster occurs, like Hurricane Matthew in 2016, we are there for those we love. You see, God had solidified an intense love for the Haitian people through years of serving in this troubled country.

Years before the tragic earthquake, my life and love of the people truly changed one day as I was sitting under a tree with a young boy. Our ministry teams had helped the village men build the first shelter in a community of mud huts. The shelter was primarily used for community gatherings, and on this occasion, it was the site of our team's mobile medical clinics. Because we had been in this particular village and gained the trust of the people who lived there, we often had people, young and old, who came to us and asked for help. Sometimes they asked for money, food, or supplies for their children's school needs. Though we try to help where appropriate, we never want the village to become dependent; rather, our focus is to create opportunities for sustainability. Though we strive for this goal, educating villagers on this issue is always difficult, and we are often inundated by people and their requests.

As my team was conducting the clinic in this shelter, I found myself sitting on a log overlooking the ocean. A little boy, whom I had known for several years, played with, and taught at vacation Bible school, came and sat with me. For the first time, Gregory failed to ask me for anything, as was his custom. Instead, he just sat on the ground next to me and rested his arm on my knee. Then a simple but remarkable thing happened. He began to pick off the dirt and trash that had accumulated on my ankles during our hike to the village. We didn't speak to each other. I didn't entertain him, and he didn't make any requests of me. He simply wanted to sit with his friend, "Pasta Bwent," for a little while.

I continued to observe the goings on at the medical clinic until I realized he had rested his head on my lap and fallen asleep. With tears in my eyes, I knew at that moment that I had a buddy now. He knew that I loved him, and he just wanted to love me back. That moment was life changing for me. It has forged the basis of our ministry's relationships within all the villages we serve in Haiti. We don't have projects; we have friends. Several months later, I was privileged to lead that young boy to Christ, and now we are brothers.

As Christians, we live by a very basic truth: "they will know us by our love." We must remember that Jesus actually touched, comforted, and healed the blind, the lame, and the leprous *before* He saved them. The church sometimes forgets this concept…that we need to love people into the kingdom.

Our ministry works alongside the local Haitian church to help feed, clothe, educate, create jobs for, and treat the physical needs of the villagers while teaching them about Jesus. By helping meet their physical needs, we gain permission to speak into their lives. What began as a project in a third-world country has produced many long-term relationships as a result of this philosophy of ministry.

One of the major flaws in the emergence of the short-term missions movement in today's evangelical church is the "project mentality." Our ministry has tried to overcome this with what we call "Days of Immersion." Our mission teams are paired with a family with whom they will spend the day. They are to enter the lives of this family and help them with everyday chores: gardening, laundry, household repairs, and child care. During this time, we encourage them to tell the family about their lives and find out about theirs, what we call "talk story." We want our teams to share their testimony and ask questions of the family. We encourage them to share their struggles, joys, and history with each other. On our building and repair projects, we tell our team members: "If you see someone sitting around while you are working, put the shovel down and go love on that person." Our goal is that our teams will develop relationships and not simply leave with a box checked off their "bucket list" of good deeds.

We find that now many team members return to Haiti, not only to accomplish the projects we have for them, but to reunite with the families with whom they worked and shared time. When those relationships have been created and cultivated, our ministry's goal of loving, serving, and truly investing in these communities has been met. We love people first and they know it. That's the key. Loving one another can't be mere words. "I love you" means nothing if you don't plan to love someone until he or she really knows it soul deep.

I Love You?

Loving one another well requires a long-term strategy. In today's complex society, we banter about words with little comprehension of their depth. In a time when we express ourselves through "thoughtful emojis" and develop relationships by instant messages and media posts, I believe we are losing a little depth to our intimacy. ☹

I believe that words have meaning. That is why I believe that we must be cautious before telling someone "I love you." Loving someone means you are committing to the relationship, be it a mate or friend, for the long haul.

There was a small group of men I met with for several years for accountability and community. I always ended our evenings by telling them I loved them. Then I'd say, "Five years." At first, I was met with puzzled looks. I had to explain that they would realize my love was real in five years' time if we were still walking through life together.

Over time we all went through tragedies, triumphs, and disappointments and experienced strains on those relationships to which we had committed. We lovingly confronted one another when one of us would fall or rebel. We mourned and celebrated with, listened to, and prayed for one another. Before the five years had elapsed I was approached by nearly all of those great guys who said, "I get it. You love me."

One of the greatest ministerial joys comes from having people I have been in community with over the years come to me and tell me that they feel loved and accepted and that there is a "net" under them that will always be there if they fall. They finally understand what the "five years" is about.

It is risky, but worth the risk. So do it. Love one another.

My challenge to you is to think about this concept the next time you tell someone "I love you." Are you agreeing to be there until they get it? Are you even willing to show your love over the long term, through all the mess and the joy, whether they get it or not? If not, you might want to rethink your words.

Loving One Another for the Long Haul

What does it mean to invest in your relationships for a long haul?

- It means not bolting from someone when that person fails you, others, or themselves.

- It means being a consistent, stable, and loyal

presence in another's life, even when you don't feel like it.

- It means being accessible for midnight calls of desperation.

- It means sacrificing _____ (fill in the blank).

- It means swallowing your pride and saying "I'm sorry" when you blow it.

- It means living with integrity—having the guts to let your yes be yes and your no be no.

- It means lovingly confronting and correcting someone, but not controlling them.

- It means being someone's biggest fan.

- It means *always*.

First Corinthians 13 is the treatise on love that everyone knows but few live out: "It *always* protects, *always* trusts, *always* hopes, *always* perseveres" (v. 7 NIV, emphasis added).

Here's a last thought about love: although it is difficult, it is well worth the hardships.

A young friend of mine continually asked those of us in his inner circle to pray for him to find the love of his life, and we did...for years. The problem was this: because of insecurity and fear of rejection, he would sabotage any relationship that moved past the initial "get to know you" stage. Soon into any romance he would begin to put up barriers in the relationship that would hinder any real intimacy. Then, when the relationship failed, he would again ask for prayer.

This cycle continued until a mutual friend and I confronted him. We explained to him that we would not continue to pray as we watched him build a brick wall around his heart a mile high and then throw prayers over the wall. The woman who could break through that wall would have to be a rhino! We began to pray for him to take the risk of intimacy, the risk of truly loving someone enough to let her in. Yes, there might be pain; actually, I can pretty much guarantee there will be. But I believe we never truly grow without pain.

It is risky, but worth the risk. So do it. Love one another. Nothing truly worth having is without sacrifice and pain. Just ask Jesus.

Exhort One Another

"Take care, brothers, lest there be in any of you an evil, unbelieving heart, leading you to fall away from the living God. But exhort one another every day, as long as it is called 'today,' that none of you may be hardened by the deceitfulness of sin."
(Hebrews 3:12-13)

Take a moment right now and close your eyes. Think of someone in your life who urged you on to be a better person. Maybe it was a teacher who said you would graduate with honors when all the other teachers said you talked too much. (Yes, that was me. Thanks, Ms. Verhagen). The person who told you it was OK to be bad for a while as you learned to play baseball. The late Bob Warren mentored me for two years and freed me from guilt over my pre-Christ life by telling me, "God didn't call you to be an imitation of Bob Warren, Brent; He wants you to be you! But He wants you to be you *for* Him."

Exhort is another one of those words that is commonly used in Christian circles but few can define. For those who have not grown up in the church, there may be a number of words and phrases that are unfamiliar. *Webster's Dictionary* defines *exhort* in this way: "to try to influence [someone] by words or advice: to strongly urge [someone] to do something."

The church has responded to this calling in a number of ways in the last few decades. In the 1980s, we all had discipleship groups. In the 1990s, we had accountability partners and mentors. Now we have small groups, core groups, "D" groups, or people we "do life" with. I'm not sure I want someone to simply "do life" with, which sounds a bit passive to me. I need someone who will come alongside me and push me when I need to be pushed. I need someone to love me when I fail. I propose to you that what we need are exhorters in our lives.

The Greek word for *exhort* is *Parakaleo*: *Para*—"to the side/alongside" and *Kaleo*—"to call." Therefore, to exhort is to call to your side. But those who are called to your side are not just there to walk with you. They will be there to prod you, encourage you, and correct your course along the way. Exhorters are not yes-men. They are not simply account-ability partners who appear only when you have scheduled a meeting, a study, or a small-group time. Exhorters are ac-tively involved in your life.

Let me pause for a moment to reveal this one significant truth about myself: I am a whiner. Even though I have the greatest job in the world, I often find myself griping about a perceived wrong, or I start to feel sorry for myself because I get overwhelmed. When I start down this road of self-pity, I find myself talking to one of my best friends and exhorters, Cathy. I remember one particular time a number of years ago when I was going on and on about some challenges before me. After my diatribe was over, Cathy paused for a moment, then looked me in the eye and said these words: "Are you done yet? Because the rest of us are sitting at the cross waiting for you to return." She was (in her not-so-gentle way) exhorting me to turn away from the fleshly feel-ings that were sidetracking me and reminding me to return to the path that would lead me back to the Spirit.

Sometimes the words of an exhorter will sting. Other times they will be like music to your ears. Because some-times you need a hug and sometimes you need a swift kick. An exhorter is that person who has permission to do both in your life. Though it has been said before, it is still aston-ishing to realize that in this world where your Facebook can update your Twitter with your Instagram picture that you will post on Pinterest, then text your friend the link immediately in order to watch the video of you posting (whew!), we are still a disconnected generation. If you want to see an example of that, go to any coffeehouse in America and observe people sitting directly across from each other, yet communicating electronically to everyone but the person with whom he or she came.

A close married couple I know shared an example of this in their own lives. They were sitting in a room together, each on their own laptop, updating blogs, checking Facebook, and such. The wife, sitting not fifteen feet away from her husband, sent him an Instant Message telling him she was hungry and saying that if he was hungry, she would meet him in the kitchen for a quick snack.

In contrast, to exhort someone, by its own definition, demands constant contact. Hebrews 3:13 says, "As long as it is called 'today.' " One old theologian described that as being "perpetually present." This is where the art of exhortation breaks down in most relationships. People are not willing to make this kind of investment in intimacy. Because life is not always a smooth ride, and sometimes there are mountains to climb, you need people to climb with you.

I spoke at a college retreat in the mountains. The students were all given large rocks (according to their size), representing their burdens, and they were instructed—as a group—to climb a mountain. They found that no one could climb alone with their rocks, their "burdens." In order for everyone to reach the final destination, they occasionally had to hand their burden to someone else and be pulled up. Finding someone in your life who will help you overcome your "mountain" is no easy task. And being that person requires patience, honesty, and truth. That is why this is one of the hardest "anothers," as we will discover when we discuss bearing with one another.

Exhorters also warn you. Look back at the rest of Hebrews 3:13: "That none of you may be hardened by the deceitfulness of sin." Many young Christians will fall away if they don't have exhorters in their lives. When I first turned my life to Christ, no one warned me about dry spells. I was not warned that the "shekinah glory" of my conversion would fade, and I would fake it just as Moses did. They also never warned me that I would be put on the front lines of a battle when I was ordained in the ministry. I didn't know I was going to be shot at by the enemy always in front of me *and* by friendly fire (the church) from behind.

I preached at a military base one time and inadvertently became part of a drill. I was told to get under some desks and men with guns came and stood at the door. I asked what was happening and was told they were having a contingency drill. The military trains for as many possible contingencies as they can. The church should be just as diligent to prepare and exhort young believers for the struggles they will face in their walk with Christ.

A young man I will call Jack came to my weekly Bible studies. He had left a very party-filled lifestyle that included drugs, alcohol, and casual sex. Having experienced that lifestyle myself, I had both been down that road and the road he was presently on, in which he was growing in Christ. One night I received a call at 3:00 a.m. from a hungover Jack who had fallen back into his old patterns. I sensed a panic within him and let him know that I was not surprised by his fall, and neither was God. This was a comfort to him because I reminded him that I told him a fall might occur. I explained that he had tripped and fallen. I encouraged him to get up and reminded him that there is no condemnation in Christ. I told him this was merely a bump in the road, and he needed to repent and start again. I exhorted him not to give Satan any more "minutes." Satan had victory in the minute of temptation and in the minutes of sin, but he should not allow him minutes of accusation or condemnation because there is no condemnation in Christ Jesus.

When toddlers are learning to walk, they constantly fall. If a parent freaks out every time the toddler falls, the toddler will learn to panic at every fall. A good parent will make a happy noise or joke with every fall. They will say, "Safe!" like an umpire behind the plate at a baseball game. Those were the words my friend Jack needed to hear when he experienced his bump in the road.

An exhorter spurs you on. Exhorters don't just give a pep talk; they show you a light at the end of the tunnel and then show you that the light of Christ doesn't just wait for you there. He comes down that tunnel to meet you where you are. When an exhorter speaks encouragement or rebuke, that person speaks with authority and power because he or she speaks the truths of the Scriptures. The apostle Paul was that kind of exhorter to the church of his time. In his letters of instruction to the churches like Ephesians, Galatians, Philippians, and probably the Letter to the Hebrews, he was, at times, lovingly correcting and encouraging, but in other instances we see him harshly rebuking. Yes, he was the churches' biggest fan, but he was never afraid to call people to righteousness and to run "the race that is set before us" (Hebrews 12:1). Paul was an excellent example of exhortation for the church.

So how can we truly exhort? To begin, we need to be sure that we are always speaking God's Word, His promises, and His precepts. God's Word is a lamp unto your feet and a light unto your path (see Psalm 119:105). Therefore, when we exhort one another, we should always be careful to use God's words more than our own words.

Remember:

- "All Scripture is breathed out by God and profit-able for teaching" (2 Timothy 3:16).

- Speak to "one another in all wisdom, singing psalms and hymns and spiritual songs" (Colossians 3:16).

- "For the word of God is living and active, sharper than any two-edged sword" (Hebrews 4:12).

Let me share one last thought on exhortation. Some people believe they do not possess the gift of exhortation. But I believe all Christians have the ability to come alongside someone and speak truth into their lives, because those of us who have the Spirit of God are filled with the *Parakletos*, which is another form of the Greek *Parakaleo* we mentioned earlier.

> *Parakletos*: Summoned, called to one's side; one who pleads and intercedes; a helper.[1]

This derivative of the root word *Parakaleo* in this instance refers to the Advocate in the form of the Holy Spirit. John 14:26 says, "But the Advocate [*Parakletos*], the Holy Spirit, whom the Father will send in my name, will teach you all things and will remind you of everything I have said to you" (NIV).

It is knowing when to touch, when to speak soothing words, and when to finally say, "Get off your mat and walk."

So here is my encouragement to you who may feel unqualified, timid, or ill equipped to be an exhorter. I believe that if you have the Holy Spirit, you have the gift of exhortation in you. Walk in the Spirit, and you are walking in the "come alongside" Spirit. So I exhort you to go and be the exhorter God intends you to be and the exhorter the church of this time desperately needs.

Comfort One Another

"Blessed be the God and Father of our Lord Jesus Christ, the Father of mercies and God of all comfort, who comforts us in all our affliction, so that we may be able to comfort those who are in any affliction, with the comfort with which we ourselves are comforted by God." (2 Corinthians 1:3-4)

All things that God gives us, we are to give to others. And that is true of comfort as well. God tells us to pour out comfort and comfort one another, just as He comforts us. But what is comfort? How does it work? I must honestly admit that I don't really have a good working definition of what "comfort one another" means. Understanding how to do that is still a work in progress for me. But here is what I know so far: though Jesus could have raised Lazarus from the dead, He cried because of the death of Lazarus. He cried for those He loved who were mourning. He mourned with them even though He knew He could, and would, totally eliminate their pain by bringing Lazarus back to life. Though many of us cry out for resurrection of our loved ones, I have yet to see that miracle in my lifetime. But people have mourned with me just as Jesus mourned with others.

During the time of my dad's death, the searing pain I experienced could not be alleviated short of a resurrection like Lazarus. But that was not God's will. I had to endure it. No one could take the pain away. So in light of that truth, that we are not capable of removing anyone's pain, how are we to comfort one another?

As we learned earlier, the truth is that we, as wounded healers, are well suited to be comforters. A comforter creates a healing atmosphere and provides a hedge of protection around the wound while God does the healing. I have been fortunate that during times of death, loss, failure, and betrayal, I had a close group of comforters who allowed me to mourn, cry, and rail at God and everyone around me. They created a safe place for me. I did not have to edit my feelings, but could express them freely without fear of judgment or condemnation.

There is no wrong way to grieve and feel hurt or pain, except one: to bottle it up and not let it out. We all need to be able to gnash our teeth and kick the walls. We need to feel the pain and express the pain, and then we can move toward getting over the pain.

To comfort one another doesn't mean you have to be the one to say all the right things. It does mean you should create a safe zone for someone to sit and say all the wrong things. It means creating that healing atmosphere where the gnashing and kicking can take place. As a comforter, what comes out of your eyes and your touch is far more important and comforting than what comes out of your mouth.

I cannot define comfort, but I can tell you what it feels

like and what it requires of a person. Comfort requires discernment, wisdom, and the leadership of the Holy Spirit. It is knowing when to touch, when to speak soothing words, and when to finally say, "Get off your mat and walk."

It will often require you to get out of your comfort zone to comfort others. Your friends won't always ask for help. You may have to be intrusive. You will need to go past the "how are you" stage and be willing to get into the nitty-gritty with them. In Paul's Second Letter to the Corinthians, he thanks the church and Titus for coming to comfort him in Macedonia. Titus entered Paul's life during a time of great trouble, fear, and even danger during his travels. Titus injected himself into the middle of Paul's fears to bring comfort at just the right time and with exactly what he apparently needed (see 2 Corinthians 7:5-7).

Truth be known, only the Holy Spirit can tell you how to truly comfort someone. Perhaps that is why it is so hard to nail down a finite definition of the word *comfort*. To comfort someone will mean different things to different people in different situations. While we have general guidelines from the Word and can look at the example of Jesus to know what our possible responses might be, we must be walking in the Spirit, staying tuned into God's leading, so we will know what to say and when to say it. The Spirit of God, the Comforter Himself, will work through us and empower us to fulfill the role of comforter to others.

Let me *love* you enough to *exhort* you to move on to the next chapter. Let me offer *comfort* to you now because these "anothers" are going to get tougher from here.

NOTE

1. The word origin of *Parakaleo* (Strong's #3870) is *Para* (Strong's #3844) and *Kaleo* (Strong's #2564).

So What?

Meditate on the following Scripture.

> A new commandment I give to you, that you love one
> another: just as I have loved you, you also are to love
> one another. By this all people will know that you are
> my disciples, if you have love for one another.
> (John 13:34-35)

- After reading this chapter, what "another" do
  you have the most trouble with in your own life?
  Loving another? Exhorting another? Comforting
  another? Explain.

- Has God brought you into situations to teach you these lessons more than once? Write your experiences below.

- Taking an honest look at how you think others perceive you, do people know you are God's disciple by your love? If not, how would you be described by others?

Do you agree or disagree with this statement: Loving someone means you are committing to the relationship for the long haul. _____ Agree _____Disagree

- Explain your answer.

- Write the name of one person in your life who you feel is in it for the long haul with you?

- Has there been conflict with that person? How did you get past the conflict? Has there been disappointment? Recall how you overcame it.

- Write the name of a person who you think needs that kind of love from you. What steps will you take to reach out to that person?

- Define the word *exhort* in your own words.

- Who is someone in your life you consider an exhorter? How has the Lord used him or her to spur you on in your life? Write below any specific words or actions from the person who motivated you.

- Are you willing to invest in someone's life in order to exhort them? Consider who that person is and describe how you can become an exhorter in his or her life.

- Explain what the word *comfort* means to you and what creates a healing atmosphere.

- Describe a time when you needed comfort. Was someone there for you? How did he or she comfort you?

- Describe some attributes or skills a comforter might need (such as patience).

- Ask God to open your eyes to those around you who need love, exhortation, or comfort. Ask Him to give you a burning desire to pour yourself out to them and the wisdom to point them to God in the process.

- What is your one main takeaway from this chapter?

Now What?

Think about specific people you love. Are you willing to go the distance with them? Before the end of this week call or make plans to spend time with at least one. Share with him or her your feelings and that you intend to be there through life's ups and downs.

Recall those who have offered comfort to you in one way or another. How did their ministry affect you? Send a note or e-mail of thanks this week.

Consider those around you who need to be comforted. How can you let the Holy Spirit lead you to comfort others? Reach out to those people this week and ask the questions below. Be prepared to follow through with that action.

Do you want to talk?

How can I help you?

How can I pray for you?

Chapter Five

THE TOUGH STUFF

Above all, love each other deeply, because love covers over a multitude of sins.
(1 Peter 4:8 NIV)

When I read that Scripture, as well as references like Galatians 6:1 that states we should restore someone with a "spirit of gentleness," my first thought is that none of this comes easy to me. And so, I place the following "anothers" in the "tough stuff" category.

We all want to be world changers. We love sermons and books that challenge us to do *great* things for God. We think we will have no problem with surrendering to a calling that involves huge plans and ridiculous sacrifices. We want to go to a third-world country on a mission. We want to trek into the jungle to reach a lost people group. That sounds easy.

But what we won't do are the small, difficult things. Maintaining relationships with our brothers and sisters in

Christ. Serving those we love with consistent compassion. Humbling ourselves and offering a nonjudgmental, noncritical, silent shoulder to cry on. These are the things that make us want to bolt.

Bear with One Another

Be completely humble and gentle; be patient, bearing with one another in love.
Ephesians 4:2 NIV

The act of bearing with someone requires an investment of time, energy, patience, forgiveness, and tolerance. It is an investment many of us are not prepared to make. The word *prepared* is the key.

We live in a society where life is mobile and therefore we can be shallow. We can move easily from friend to friend, relationship to relationship, and never truly know each other. In early American society, the average person was born, raised, lived, and died in the same town. Because of this, people had to live together in community, share one another's burdens, and work out differences. Today, because of our thin ties to those around us, we are not prepared, because we have not had to experience "long-suffering" with anyone. This has resulted in families becoming disconnected, divorces increasing, and churches splitting, all because we lack the basic skill of "bearing with one another."

In order to develop the skills to bear with one another, we need to understand that, in Scripture, there are two types of burdens and two types of bearing.

Galatians 6:2 says, "Bear ye one another's burdens, and so fulfil the law of Christ" (KJV). The word *burden* in this Scripture carries with it the idea of a load that is too heavy for just one person to carry alone. At some point in the life of every person, the strains of life can become too much. This is when a Christian needs to become the "burden lifter" God intends us to be. This is when we are to bear the burden for our friend.

The prevailing thought in modern times, especially in many "first-world" cultures, is that "their problem is not my responsibility." Yet Paul's words contradict this way of thinking in one simple word: *brethren*. This word begins chapter 6 of his Letter to the Galatians. The word *brother* meant something in that day and time. In many societies today, such as the Haitian culture of which I am familiar, the family unit is still very intact and in many ways holds the same family values as in the time of Paul. In these cultures, it is expected that a family is responsible for the well-being and education of all its members—even to the extended family. The family unit helps meet all needs.

This family responsibility concept has faded in many societies. In fact, it sounds absurd to many to think that we are responsible for the education and material needs of our brothers, sisters, cousins, and their children. But this was the case in Paul's culture. Paul was reminding the church that in the family of God, we are all brothers and sisters. Therefore, we are obligated to serve one another. This idea of bearing someone's burden means to lift up, take off, and sometimes even carry away. That is how we are to treat our brothers and sisters in Christ.

I saw this concept of "burden bearing" fleshed out at my own church in an amazing way. A single mother of two high school boys had become overwhelmed. She worked two jobs, had chronic back pain, and her financial burdens were too much to bear. She did the best she could, but her bills were piled high. Her credit cards were maxed out, and she had doctor bills and orthodontist bills for her kids. Feeling the Lord prompting me to help her, but not having the means to remove her financial burdens alone, I sat down with a brilliant businessman in my church. Together, we came up with a new and different idea to assist *our sister*. We gathered many single adults in our church. Each committed to "adopt" and make the minimum payments on one of her bills for one year. This freed up the money from myriad minimum payments that were drowning her, and she was able to pay down one bill at a time in order to get her finances back in shape. Because we all were able to share her burden, she was able to pay off many of the balances herself, and she was left with a feeling of accomplishment. All we did was lighten her load. Our singles ministry replicated this many times over the next few years, helping many of our brethren.

This is an example of a burden we can help bear and are supposed to help bear. The burdens of the oppressed, hurting victims of the countless evils of this world should be lifted by the children of a loving God, but there are other burdens and issues that we are not supposed to remove from our friends and family members. These are the burdens mentioned in Galatians 6:4-5: "But let every man prove his own work, and then shall he have rejoicing in himself alone, and not in another. For every man shall bear his own burden" (KJV).

This seems to contradict verse 2; however, when you explore the meanings of the words, it makes perfect sense. The word *burden* in this passage was used to describe a sack or backpack a soldier carried on a daily basis. These burdens are the ones Christ gives us to bear ourselves in order to grow us and make us stronger. I, as your brother in Christ, am not to remove this from you. I am not to bear this burden. However, I can bear with you as you carry this burden yourself.

I had the privilege of teaching at a juvenile detention center for boys outside of Nashville, Tennessee. During one of those visits, I shared Christ with a young man who had just arrived at the facility. In the midst of our conversation, he asked if God would get him out of the detention center if he gave his life to Christ. I explained that there was no way he could make a deal with God because you can only make a deal with someone if you have something the other needs. "You need Christ's forgiveness," I said, "but He needs nothing from you. He loves you and wants you, but you have nothing that He doesn't already possess." This young man

119

went on to receive God's forgiveness that night. He served his time, and during that time a group of godly men and women mentored him. They walked beside him and bore with him until his release. Even though Jesus forgave him of his sins, there were consequences to his actions, and he still owed a debt to society that he needed to pay.

In that same vein, I often get angry when I hear radio and TV commercials that say, "Are creditors hounding you? Stop the debt collection process and get rid of those credit card companies." Although I understand there are extenuating circumstances where people are faced with crippling debt through no fault of their own (such as hospitalizations and the rising cost of health care), many people make the choice to spend irresponsibly. To simply erase that debt with no consequences would accomplish nothing in that person's life. The creditors are calling because they are owed money that is not being paid. Those in that situation have the opportunity to grow and mature by responsibly paying the debt and learning a lesson of stewardship. As a friend, I will help you develop a budget, hold you accountable, and occasionally buy you dinner and a movie to give you some R & R during your financial recovery. In this way I will bear with you as you bear this burden yourself, but I am not your friend if I simply remove your debt burden with a single bank deposit.

Let's look at two Scriptures in which Paul instructs us on how to bear with each other:

- "Be completely humble and gentle; be patient, bearing with one another in love" (Ephesians 4:2 NIV).

- "Therefore, as God's chosen people, holy and dearly loved, clothe yourselves with compassion, kindness, humility, gentleness and patience. Bear with each other" (Colossians 3:12-13 NIV).

Notice the pivotal word in both of these Scriptures is *patience*. First Corinthians 13 says "love is *patient*" (v. 4, emphasis added). Galatians 5:22 says the fruit of the spirit is "love, joy, peace, and *patience*" (emphasis added). This word is oftentimes translated as "long-suffering."

Just as there are several meanings of the word *burden* in Scripture, there are several differences between the words *patience* and *long-suffering*, though both long-suffering and patience are required when bearing with one another.

The best description of *patience* that I have heard to date is "to wait hopefully with expectation." At my ordination into the ministry, which was one of the most beautiful moments of my life, right before I knelt in front of the leaders of the church, the pastor encouraged members to express thoughts and testimonies of my work at the church. During that service, a sweet, genteel southern lady stood. I had worked with her and the senior adults for years. I was moved that she was going to give testimony on my behalf. Then she said the following words with a smirk: "Brent, when you first came to this church, nobody liked you."

She went on to describe a young, impatient, and opinionated man. She then ended her testimony by saying, "We loved you and we knew you would grow." Of all the kind words I heard that night, those have remained with me, and as I write this, she and I remain very close friends. This is probably due to the fact that she has continued to patiently bear with me throughout the years.

Patience is a wonderful trait to possess and can be difficult to practice in some situations. Long-suffering, on the other hand, carries with it the elements of extended time and pain. These two factors are the reason people don't want to invest in the lives of others. It will take too much time and may be painful. Long-suffering continues when patience runs out. When we don't invest in the long haul with someone, we miss out on the benefits of those relationships. The testimony of a marriage that has lasted for forty or fifty years is a beautiful example of long-suffering, but not in a negative light. Instead, it is symbolic of the couple's ability to withstand hardships and tragedies by clinging to each other in the darkest times and celebrating achievements in their joyous times.

Let's return to 1 Corinthians 13 (the "love" chapter). This unpacks the words *patience* and *long-suffering* when it says love "*always* protects, *always* trusts, *always* hopes, *always* perseveres" (v. 7 NIV, emphasis added). Love *never* fails. Bearing one another's burdens and bearing with one another will require an *always* and *never* attitude.

What relationships are you in right now that can be described with these "always and nevers"? If you have one, you are very blessed; to be in one requires work and commitment. But know this: the benefits of a lifelong relationship with someone who both "bears your burdens" and "bears with you" are immeasurable.

Forgive One Another

Be kind to one another, tenderhearted,
forgiving one another, as God in Christ
forgave you. (Ephesians 4:32)

"But really, God...seventy times seven?" the pupil must have asked after Jesus's instruction on how many times we are to forgive (see Matthew 18:22).

I believe Christ was being metaphorical. He was painting a picture of ongoing, perpetual forgiveness. He was saying, "Break your pride, give up your right to get revenge, and forgive...over and over again." Forgiving one another is one of the most difficult tasks given by God to His children. Because sin entered the world and the heart of man has been forever tainted by "self," we are bound to hurt one another. The whole world seems to be only about fulfilling their own selfish needs first, above all things. We get our needs met at the expense of others when we should be spending our lives giving to others. We are perpetual takers. Therefore, our pride leaves pain and offense in our wake. I defy you to find a relationship between two people that has not included this kind of pain and did not require forgiveness. But the reward of a relationship that has survived the cycle of offense, pain, and forgiveness is a deeper, lasting connection that grows out of gratitude, love, and shared experiences.

The work of forgiveness does not seem to come easy, or naturally, to the average person. That is why Jesus addressed it so often in His conversations with the disciples. It also features prominently in His prayers: "Forgiving others…as God has forgiven you" (Luke 6:37, paraphrased; see also Matthew 6:9-15; Mark 11:25).

Mountains and Molehills

We have all heard the old statement, "You're making a mountain out of a molehill." And though the person speaking that barb to you might not mean to do anything but infuriate you, there is wisdom in it. The truth is, we encounter both mountains and molehills in our relationships, both large and small offenses that require forgiveness. But these might take different methods of accomplishing forgiveness. So I believe it's important to explore these two kinds of offenses and define some of these mountains and molehills in our lives.

Molehills

It's a fact that everyone will be offended, and everyone will hurt someone else in his or her lifetime. Whether it is a snide remark, unintentional neglect, or we are rubbed the wrong way by the personality of another, we will experience friction in relationships.

Countless relationships, friendships, and marriages have been ruined because of one phenomenon: they moved in together. "He leaves the seat up." "She changes the channel." "He is so inconsiderate." "She uses all the hot water." The list goes on and on. Those small issues can lead to the destruction of a relationship if they go unchecked. How should we deal with these small but not insignificant problems?

As a homeowner in Tennessee, I am often at war with and annoyed by those destructive little rodents called moles. They love to burrow just under the surface of the grass or in the garden, searching for worms and grubs. In their wake they leave behind hills and tunnels all over the place. Many mornings I have enjoyed my coffee while stomping down the molehills in the yard. One of the things I've learned from my morning missions is that you don't have to "get over" a molehill. There's nothing to climb. You merely stomp down these little annoying disturbances to your otherwise beautiful landscape before they affect the root system of what you've planted.

True forgiveness is whiting out both sides of the page.

Let me offer some methods and thoughts on steps to stomp the molehills.

First, define these molehill offenses as what they are in their basest form: small stuff. Determine whether a particular offense is a deal breaker in the relationship. Is it a dragon that will devour all of your good feelings toward that person, all of the love or goodwill? Or is this just an annoying gnat that merely irritates? Ask the question, "Is winning this argument worth more than the value of the relationship?"

My father used to tell me not to sweat the small stuff and to learn how to pick my battles—clichés that are truly good advice. Stop looking at the gnat as a dragon. We get into a trap when we obsess over things and try to micromanage one another's lives. We lose focus and perspective. If I intend to focus on the faults of another person, I can find a myriad of things to become upset about. But is damaging the relationship, either friendship or marital union, worth it? The question needs to be, "How important is this relationship to me?"

Here's an exercise. Ask yourself, "How much do I value this relationship in my life? What is it worth?" If this is a $10K relationship, am I going to trade it for the $2 reward of simply winning the argument? When you realize another person's worth, you will see that most quarrels and offenses don't warrant the time and energy you are spending on them. It's then that the cost of forgiving that person will seem like pocket change.

Second, find the "because" behind the offense. I am a hopeless optimist. I believe that few people go into a relationship wanting to hurt the other person. But sooner or later, we will hurt one another. Why is that?

The answer to that question can often be the beginning of healing and forgiveness.

There is always a "because." There is a *reason* most people react to their environment instead of being proactive in their interactions with others. They are acting as a consequence of how they were treated in the past and what they expect of the relationship. People abuse because they have been abused. People lie because they have been lied to or to protect themselves, or they attempt to impress in order to raise their horrible self-esteem. Though it may be difficult to decipher sometimes, try to see your offender from another angle. When the person who has victimized you becomes a victim in your mind, it is easier to begin to forgive him or her.

Sometimes a person lashes out in order to protect his or her own heart. As my "brick wall" friend from the last chapter said to me, "I've been hurt before and will never love again." Because of this wall, he had become aloof, insensitive, cynical, sarcastic, and defensive to anyone who tried to get close to him. Most people saw him as a jerk and would write him off and be offended in most any interaction with him. It took looking behind the wall to see he was an awesome young man with a great sense of humor and a heart for poor and hurting people.

It takes someone who is willing to make the investment to break through some of these walls and get to forgiveness and understanding to build a relationship.

The third and most difficult method to deal with molehill offenses is the "Liquid Paper" method. In ancient times, before the Delete button on a laptop, there were archaic machines called typewriters. In order to correct typographical mistakes, one had to use a concoction that a woman named Bette Nesmith Graham created in her kitchen. That concoction was called Liquid Paper. This was a magical liquid elixir used by the gallons in universities and offices around the world. Liquid Paper had only one drawback: once it was applied and blotted out the mistake on the paper, all one had to do to see the original mistake was to turn the paper over. If the paper was thin, you could clearly see what had been written. To truly conceal from your boss or professor your less-than-stellar work, you would have to use Liquid Paper to cover up both sides of the paper.

Let's say a person offends me. In an effort to restore the relationship, I say, "I forgive you" and we walk away as great friends, right? Wrong! I probably said that I forgive him or her with my words, but in reality, I take that offense and put it in my back pocket to use against that person later. I add it to the list of offenses that were supposedly forgiven in the past. But I know that list is at my fingertips, ready to pull out and use against him or her at any time in the future.

The Liquid Paper method is the secret of forgiveness. You have to blot the transgression out completely. It has to become more than simple words. True forgiveness is covering up both sides of the page.

Any good marital or relational counselor will teach a couple to honor rules with regard to arguments. One of the most important guidelines is that bringing up past offenses is against the rules. It is not going to mean you forget the offense; it means you can't use the offense against the other person. You have to empty your pockets of all the grudges you are holding on to. You have to cover up both sides of the page. This gives the person who offended you the grace to grow and change. It also means you are not keeping someone in constant debt to you. Just like the Scripture says, a debtor is always a slave to the lender (Isaiah 24:2). So is there any person in your life you have not forgiven because you feel he or she still owes you? Forgive that person. Free him or her of this debt, and free yourself in the process.

Climb Every Mountain

What about the mountains? There comes a time in the life of many relationships where a seemingly acidic or massive betrayal of trust, something like an affair or a theft, occurs. This is when a relationship may look destined to be severed. The hurt and offense go soul deep. These "mountains" seem impassable, and many people will fall into depression or despair thinking they can never overcome the damage that has occurred. These situations require an amazing act of forgiveness that only God can bring about.

One of the first things to tackle and realize in the process of forgiveness of these heinous acts is the destructive nature of unforgiveness. The writer in Hebrews 12:15 warns us about developing a "root of bitterness." He goes on to tell the reader that it will defile many. That unforgiveness rarely affects the offender is a sobering thought. However, it can completely destroy the victim and hurt others in that victim's path. A person who refuses to forgive stays perpetually a victim to that offense and will never be victorious over it.

> *Of all the instructions Christ has given His followers, submission comes closest to being Christlike than any other.*

Your body is an amazing thing. The same chemicals and endorphins that make up the fight-or-flight reflexes can be triggered by your memory, thus increasing your blood pressure and anxiety. When you don't forgive someone, your mind can replay the offense and your body can be affected. That's why the old statement rings true: "Forgiveness is a gift you give yourself." Why are you allowing that person to hurt you repeatedly, every time you replay the offense? If you release him or her, you will actually free yourself. In understanding this concept, you can begin the process of healing in your life.

I want to caution that in no way do I mean to diminish and trivialize the pain that someone has gone through. These are merely suggestions. Let God apply them to the heart as He works through your situation.

It's also important to note that you should be a welcome mat, but not a doormat. Forgiving someone does not mean allowing someone to hurt you again. You are not a doormat to be repeatedly stepped on. Though I am to forgive seventy times seven times, I am not to throw myself in front of the oncoming train so I can forgive the engineer over and over. To be a welcome mat means to be willing to do the work of restitution and reconciliation.

However, in certain instances, such as theft, betrayal, and even in the case of marital unfaithfulness, the victim has had something taken, either physically or emotionally. And the obvious beginning of reconciliation in these cases is repentance and restitution.

The physical restitution is the easy part. Returning the value of a stolen item or the item itself is easy. Repaying an emotional debt is much more costly. Restoring the trust that has been broken is not as simple as writing a check. It is not wrong or a sign of unwillingness to forgive in certain cases to require that someone establish a path of regaining the lost trust. For many, it will require a certain amount of time and intentional effort to regain the trust of the betrayed. The woman who has been cheated on has the right to expect her husband to seek counseling and set accountability measures in his life. The embezzler should, after repaying the debt, allow accountability and complete transparency in any transactions he or she initiates afterward. It is not harsh or a sign of an unwillingness to forgive to ask someone to rebuild that trust with you. This is the work of reconciliation.

I must reiterate here that this does not mean becoming a doormat. In fact, there are some cases (such as abuse or issues relating to addictions) where there would be actual danger in restoring the relationship. In these cases, a person can experience the healing of forgiving the offender without restoring contact with that person.

Now, I must concede here that there are simply some mountains, some offenses, you cannot overcome through some prescribed method no matter how well you follow it. But there is an answer in Scripture: "I say to you, if you have faith like a grain of mustard seed, you will say to this mountain, 'Move from here to there,' and it will move, and nothing will be impossible for you" (Matthew 17:20). During these times I believe that our God can perform a true "mountain-moving miracle."

An example of the miraculous miracles I've experienced occurred in the days preceding my father's death. I have never experienced such tension and pain in such an extended period of time as I watched his body struggle for each breath. On the night of his death, I stood over him and said to God, "I know you can heal Him. If you are waiting for me to have faith, I have seen what you can do." I had seen miracles occur. I knew God could heal my father. At that moment, I can truly say I believe God spoke to me very clearly. His answer was no.

But then, in my heart I felt Him saying this: "The answer is no, Brent, but here is *a peace that passes understanding*." It was one of the most supernatural moments I have ever experienced. A complete peace swept through me as my father took his last breath. I will never be able to explain it fully, but that was a peace that I could never have conjured myself. It was a gift given to me by God that sustained me from that point on.

In the same way, concerning forgiveness, there comes a point where nothing works. The pain is too searing, the agony too much. There is no earthly way to ever forgive that person for what he or she has done to you. At that moment, God can do something miraculous in your life. I believe He can give you the grace of forgiveness *that passes all under-standing*. So ask God for that miracle. We have all heard the stories of family members of a murdered person who go to the prison and forgive the murderer. It is only by the very nature of God that this grace can be given through us when we walk in the Spirit of God.

So, whether by method or miracle, find the grace to forgive. Forgiveness is absolutely essential in the life of every Christian who intends to lose himself for the sake of knowing Christ and the depth of a fulfilled life of pouring out to others. We must break our pride, give up "our rights," and lavish grace and forgiveness on those around us so that we can be filled with His love and grace ourselves.

Submit to One Another

"Submitting to one another out of reverence for Christ."
Ephesians 5:21

Just as the biggest hindrance to forgiveness is pride, so it is with the next "another": submission. Of all the instructions Christ has given His followers, submission comes closest to being Christlike than any other.

In Philippians 2, we see the essence of Christ's character. Scriptures like verse 8 tell us, "And being found in appearance as a man, he humbled himself by becoming obedient to death—even death on a cross!" (NIV). When we submit to one another, there is no selfish ambition, no vain conceit. Paul says that we should live a life that counts others more significant than yourself and looks not only to your own interests but also to the interests of others. He also reminds us that He "emptied himself, by taking on the form of a servant" (v. 7). So, as Paul tells us in verse 5, "In your relationships with *one another*, have the same mindset as Christ Jesus" (NIV, emphasis added).

Let's take the word *submit* back to its Greek origin. The word in the Greek is *Hupotasso*, which means "to arrange or assign under." Though few people will admit it, it is not uncommon to enter into a room of people and subconsciously arrange people according to their "rank." This applies to whatever situation we find ourselves in, be it wealth, physical appearance, or employer/employee.

At this point, the politically correct view would be to talk about how wrong and unfair this ranking would be. But if we instead apply the biblical truth of submission, this prejudice would be resolved. To submit simply means that no matter the rank of the people in the room, I arrange myself at the bottom. I consciously determine to humble myself and consider others better than myself. I truly believe if people would adopt this philosophy, it would curb many of our world's issues like racism, gender inequality, and marital conflicts.

When the word *submission* is brought up, one of the first topics of controversy people mention is in the area of marriage. But even in an initial reading of the marriage

Scriptures in Ephesians 5:22-33, it is apparent that Paul is talking about *mutual* submission. It is as if he takes the women into another room and tells the women in the room to submit to their husbands. In the same way, he calls a special meeting with the men to tell them they are to love their wives as Christ loved the church. Paul finishes this marital discourse in verses 31-33 by saying, "The two shall become one flesh" and by urging the husband to "love his wife as himself, and let the wife see that she respects her husband." That is a beautiful picture of mutual submission.

Ephesians 5 has often been twisted to justify marital abuse and even slavery. But I humbly submit to you this: the very nature of the word *submit* dispels those distortions because submission can never be demanded. It must be freely given. It is assigned by the giver. If it is demanded by the authority, it becomes subjugation or oppression.

Submission is the calling of every Christian. This truth flies in the face of all that we hold dear, especially in the United States. We have a society that demands its rights all the time. This is why a true follower of Christ will be set apart from those around him or her. And that's a good thing. One who emulates Jesus will be set aside from others in the world by his or her actions and how he or she lives so differently, and that person will have the ability to speak into the lives of others around him or her. This is why God calls us to be holy as He is holy.

Holy = set apart for special service.

135

The flesh exalts itself and demands that everything around it exalt it as well. Our flesh demands its right for self-fulfillment. Thus, the challenge is to overcome the flesh or to crucify the flesh as "those who belong to Christ Jesus" (Galatians 5:24).

I am always amazed when I consider the last physical days of the life of Christ. The King of kings, the Son of the One True God, who was God, allowed Himself to be arrested, beaten, spat upon, and humiliated. It's been said that on the day of His crucifixion, one of the most amazing miracles Jesus performed was the miracle of His restraint. Jesus Himself said that He could call down legions of angels. With that kind of angel army, He could have wiped the human race from the planet and began again. Instead, He submitted to the will of His Father, to the point of the nail and thrust of the spear, without putting up a fight.

When you find yourself working underneath an unfair supervisor you disagree with or are serving with a pastor or church leader with a negative and unkind spirit, or even in a marriage where it is difficult to submit to your spouse, think on these things and realize you have not yet truly suffered. The ultimate act of submission by Christ released the unfathomable power of grace that we still benefit from today. What will your act of submission release into the lives of those around you?

So What?

Meditate on the following Scripture.

> Above all, keep loving one another earnestly, since love covers a multitude of sins. Show hospitality to one another without grumbling. As each has received a gift, use it to serve one another, as good stewards of God's varied grace: whoever speaks, as one who speaks oracles of God; whoever serves, as one who serves by the strength that God supplies—in order that in everything God may be glorified through Jesus Christ. To Him belong glory and dominion forever and ever. Amen. (1 Peter 4:8-11)

- Review the two types of burdens mentioned in chapter 5. Reflect on a time when the burdens you bore were too heavy for you. Did you reach out for help? How?

- Give an example of someone who came along during this journey. How did the Lord use him or her to help you bear this burden?

- There are some burdens we must bear alone. What is the difference between the two burdens mentioned in this chapter? What burdens do you bear that you believe have been given to make you stronger?

Ask God to open your eyes to the burdened people around you. Ask the Lord to give you the wisdom to know when to lift those burdens that need to be lifted and when to be there to bear with those that need to grow from the burdens they must bear.

- Is there anyone who has forgiven you? How did this situation play out and how can you use it as a learning experience in the future?

- What is the difference between a mountain and a molehill when it comes to forgiveness? Have you found it difficult to cover up the transgression?

- Think of someone who has committed a molehill offense against you. Ask yourself how much that relationship is worth to you. Ten dollars? Ten thousand? Ask yourself how much it will cost to forgive and get over this offense. Is it worth holding this debt against them? Ask God to help you forgive them and cover up the offense to restore your relationship.

- How badly do you cringe when you hear the word submission? Why do you think this word has such negative connotations?

- Who should you submit to in your life? How is it going? If you find this a difficult task, why? Ask the Lord to remove the barriers to your submission to that person now.

- Remember a time when you entered a room and "ranked" other people? What ranking measure did you use? Where did you place yourself in that rank? Write down the situation and then imagine how the event would have played out differently if you had ranked yourself at the bottom.

- What is your one main takeaway from this chapter?

Now What?

Has God brought someone into your life who needs help with a burden? Make a plan to help that person now.

Did God bring someone to mind during your reading that you need to forgive? Begin to say out loud, "I forgive you." If you need to contact him or her, do it. If you need a little help in the process of forgiving that person, seek a counselor, minister, or friend to help walk you through this difficult task.

THE HOW-TO'S

THE HEART OF THE FATHER

See what kind of love the Father has given to us, that we should be called children of God; and so we are.

1 John 3:1

U p until now, we have been focusing on methods and philosophies of living "another" life. However, if you are like me, you need to see something from many angles in order for this concept to truly sink in past your head and into your heart. How is this kind of life truly fleshed out? We are going to look at this from three different angles. Let us first look at the heart of God.

As I wrote in the first chapter, Christians are grafted into the vine of Christ. So, what's true about the Vine is now true about us. God is the vine and you are the branches. When you become a Christian, you are given a new heart and are now connected directly to the heart of God. Because He intends to live His life through us, I think it's a good idea to explore the heart of our Father to give us insight into our relationship with God and how we are to respond to one another.

As I travel and speak to various groups, I get excited when people come to know the Lord for the first time. They have an energy and enthusiasm for what the Lord has done to save them. I also have the opportunity to speak with people in various stages of their Christian walk—those whose walk is Spirit-led, as well as those who have become weighed down with sin and feel as if they have fallen away or that they have gone too far for too long and question their relationship with God.

Those in the latter group often ask if I believe the Lord will still love and accept them, given their spiritual state. I have realized, for these believers, it is not a question of accepting Christ; it is the *acceptance of* Christ that is weighing them down. They desperately need someone to tell them that there is no condemnation in Christ Jesus, but it's in this loving task that we Christians often fail.

Jesus understood that we would struggle with this, and so He spoke often on the nature of God and His love. Jesus often tried to explain to His disciples and the teachers of the law about the heart of His Father. And there is no better place to see the giving, loving heart of the Father that we now possess than in His parable of the Prodigal Father (see Luke 15:11-32).

Jesus told this story while He was at a Pharisee's house where He was being watched closely by many of the teachers of the law. His treatment of sinners, the sick, and the Sabbath was so radically different that He caused some serious rumblings among the religious elite. So Jesus took that moment to explain the heart of God to those lawgivers who condemned Him as well as to His constantly confused disciples.

He began by teaching three parables: the lost coin (about a woman who searched and searched for a lost coin and threw a big party when she found it), the lost sheep (about a shepherd who left his flock to search for one that was lost and then rejoiced when it was found), and the prodigal son (about a son who lost his way and the father who welcomed him home with open arms). I think we've mistakenly refocused those stories on what was lost, when there was a bigger lesson Jesus wanted us to see.

The parable of the lost coin had nothing to do with the "lostness" of the coin—how it got in that condition and how it found its way back. It was about the extravagant effort the woman went to in order to find it and the party she threw when she did. Jesus did not focus on the "lostness" of the sheep, but on the shepherd, who would not rest until all his sheep were safe in the fold. The story of the prodigal son is more about the father who gave his son all he had, ran to his son when he returned, and welcomed his son home with a lavish display of love. The parables should be called the Extravagant Woman, the Loving Shepherd, and the Prodigal Father.

The parable of the prodigal son explains why the title of

this chapter is not a typographical error or a mistake. The definition of the word *prodigal* according to Dictionary.com includes "extravagant, giving or yielding profusely; lavish; a person who spends, or has spent, his or her money or substance with wasteful extravagance."

So, who was the extravagant one here? Who was lavishly abundant? Who was seemingly wasteful with his resources? Let's look at the passage in Luke 15:

> And he said, "There was a man who had two sons. And the younger of them said to his father, 'Father, give me the share of property that is coming to me.' And he divided his property between them. Not many days later, the younger son gathered all he had and took a journey into a far country, and there he squandered his property in reckless living. And when he had spent everything, a severe famine arose in that country, and he began to be in need. So he went and hired himself out to one of the citizens of that country, who sent him into his fields to feed pigs. And he was longing to be fed with the pods that the pigs ate, and no one gave him anything.
>
> "But when he came to himself, he said, 'How many of my father's hired servants have more than enough bread, but I perish here with hunger! I will arise and go to my father, and I will say to him, "Father, I have sinned against heaven and before you. I am no longer worthy to be called your son. Treat me as one of your hired servants."' And he arose and came to his father. But while he was still a long way off, his father saw him and

felt compassion, and ran and embraced him and kissed him. And the son said to him, 'Father, I have sinned against heaven and before you. I am no longer worthy to be called your son.' But the father said to his servants, 'Bring quickly the best robe, and put it on him, and put a ring on his hand, and shoes on his feet. And bring the fattened calf and kill it, and let us eat and celebrate. For this my son was dead, and is alive again; he was lost, and is found.' And they began to celebrate.

"Now his older son was in the field, and as he came and drew near to the house, he heard music and dancing. And he called one of the servants and asked what these things meant. And he said to him, 'Your brother has come, and your father has killed the fattened calf, because he has received him back safe and sound.' But he was angry and refused to go in. His father came out and entreated him, but he answered his father, 'Look, these many years I have served you, and I never disobeyed your command, yet you never gave me a young goat, that I might celebrate with my friends. But when this son of yours came, who has devoured your property with prostitutes, you killed the fattened calf for him!' And he said to him, 'Son, you are always with me, and all that is mine is yours. It was fitting to celebrate and be glad, for this your brother was dead, and is alive; he was lost, and is found.' "

The first thing to note is that God gives His children far more than they can ask for or deserve. When the younger, ungrateful son asked for his inheritance, he was telling his father that he, the father, was dead to him, the son, because the son had no legal right to his inheritance until after his father's death. Not only did he not have the legal right to ask

> *There is never a point that you can run away from the God who lives in you and through you.*

for his inheritance under Jewish law, but his request was the highest form of disrespect. The son deserved nothing. Yet the father sold everything he had and split his estate between his two sons. In doing that, the father was fully aware that now he himself owned nothing.

You and I do not deserve any of God's mercy and love and the riches of His kingdom. We deserve death and hell for our sins against God and one another. But God not only pours mercy on us by not punishing us, He lavishly pours grace on us and gives us Himself and heaven and all the power we will ever need in order to live an abundant life today.

Ephesians 1:7-8 says, "In him we have redemption through his blood, the forgiveness of sins, in accordance with the riches of God's grace that he lavished on us" (NIV). God pours out that unconditional love on us constantly, though none of us warrant that kind of treatment. And I am amazed by how quickly the feeling of entitlement can return over and over and over in my Christian walk. Yet all I have to do is stop, count my sins, and count His blessings to see that I am a pampered, unconditionally loved child.

Second Peter 1:3 tells us we have been given everything we need for life and godliness at our salvation. Everything. We. Need. Then why do we so quickly go looking elsewhere for fulfillment from things to give us life? We will never find life or godliness apart from Jesus. I once heard it said, "Jesus said 'it is finished,' not 'I hope this helps.'" We were made complete at the moment of our salvation. Just knowing that I lack nothing can sometimes snap me out of my selfish, wayward philosophy of life. God gives His gifts freely and gives us all we need, and we need to open our eyes to that daily.

Knowing this unconditional, lavish love of our Father should lead us to offer that same grace to those around us. Many times someone's actions toward us don't at all make us feel like loving that person back. But Jesus's mandate to us is clear: "For everyone to whom much is given, from him much will be required" (Luke 12:48b NKJV). We have been so loved, forgiven, and blessed that the only reasonable response to others should be to extend these blessings to others.

The second reason that the father in this parable is prodigal is the fact that he allowed his son to go and learn. Free will is a gift. We are not robots. A loving parent will give his or her child freedom to make decisions and make mistakes. In the same way our loving Father lets us go learn.

Parents who place too many restrictions on their children and do not allow them to learn from their mistakes will find they raise insecure, indecisive children with weak values who oftentimes stray into rebellion. I ask parents all the time whether they would rather have children who act right or choose right. The child who chooses right has to, within reason and with wisdom, be given choices in order to develop the ability and discernment to choose what is right and good. That is what a loving parent does.

When I was a toddler, standing on the front seat of my father's truck (well before seat belt laws), I told my dad that I wanted a cigar. I was a persistent child, so even though my dad repeatedly told me no, I kept badgering him for the cigar. Finally he said, "OK, son, here it is." He bit the tip off the cigar and stuck it in my mouth. After taking one or two "toddler" drags, I quickly learned that I did not want the cigar. This was further confirmed when my father had to hold my head as I was violently ill and reminded me that I was the one who asked for it. He was letting me fully understand the ramifications of my choice. The father in the prodigal story would have known the maturity of his son. He would have had at least some knowledge that his son would squander everything. But this did not stop him from giving all he had to his son.

We learn by experience that our parents were right. Oftentimes we don't learn, just as occurred with the wayward son, until our resources give out, the people we thought we could count on let us down, and everything crumbles around us. Then the loving father takes us back, bandages our wounds, and holds us close while we heal.

The father in this story was also incredibly and instantly compassionate and discerning. Luke 15:20 says, "But while he was still a long way off…" The father recognized his son the minute he saw him in the distance and knew he was coming home. In fact, even when most might not have been able to tell who it was, this father just knew that man was his son. His heart was so full of joy at the prospect of his son's return that he began to run to his son. He met his son right there on the path and immediately began restoring him to his place in the family.

I have heard it said, "I have been so far away from God, I can't go home." My question is always, "Where did you go that you were away from God?"

What a messed-up view of God we have when we think we are away from God. You never went away from Him. God sees and knows right where you are at all times. He holds every molecule of this existence together, and He is in and through it all (see Colossians 1:16-17). You are never lost to Him.

Let this truth sink in: He knew you at your worst when He saved you. In fact, for some who are reading this, it should be comforting because you are not yet at your worst. There is never a point that you can run away from the God who lives in you and through you. He will always see you even if you feel like you are far off. He will always meet you right on your path and restore you to His family.

Another Son

But Jesus's parable also speaks of the elder son, who was out in the field working when his younger brother returned.

We see a very sharp contrast between the heart of God and the heart of the returning son's brother, which was representative of the Pharisees who were listening to the story.

The elder son's reaction to his brother is significant. The older son had continued to work and serve his father while the younger one was out gallivanting around the countryside, wasting his inheritance. However, though the older one was in action doing all the "right" things, he was not serving with joy or gratitude or a heart of humility. At one point, this ungrateful child has the audacity to berate his father for rejoicing at his younger son's return. "Look! All these years I've been *slaving* for you and never disobeyed your orders. Yet you never gave me even a young goat so I could celebrate with my friends. But when this son of yours who has squandered your property with prostitutes comes home, you kill the fattened calf for him!" (Luke 15:29-30 NIV, emphasis added).

One of the first and most remarkable things to note in this passage is that the elder son considered himself to be a slave to his father. He completely forgot that his father had relinquished all rights to his own property and had divided it equally between his two sons. The father owned nothing. Everything had been given to the elder son as well. But somehow the older brother refused to live under that grace.

It is always amazing to see people who get angry when I speak about grace because they have a vested interest in their own righteousness. They are under the false idea that their works and good deeds somehow elevate them to a higher level to obtain God's love. I tell those people, "Keep trying to please God. See how that works for you." The Bible plainly states, "All our righteousnesses are like filthy rags" (Isaiah 64:6 NKJV). The best thing you've ever done for God pales in comparison to His glory! You must understand this simple truth: *God loves you for no good reason!*

Embracing God's acceptance and unconditional love is a difficult task for many. They would rather consider themselves slaves that "deserve" rather than pampered children who can only receive. These, like the elder son, are the people who become angry with God when things go wrong, and they are constantly judgmental of others, having set themselves up on their own pedestal.

> *"They will know us by our love" is only the beginning.*

Like yours, my phone rings at the most inopportune times—while checking out at the store, in the middle of a movie, the moment the waiter sets down my plate of food. Often that call is from a long-distance friend I met on the road, who is now struggling with some issues and has no one to talk to. On one of these occasions, the slow Texas drawl on the other end of the phone told me that my cowboy friend was in trouble.

"Well...I've blown it," he said, and I immediately knew what he meant. His story, like mine, was a tale full of drunkenness and debauchery, so common with people from my generation. Though he had come out of that lifestyle years earlier and had become very active in his church and in our ministry in Haiti, he had, once again, slipped into a party lifestyle and had been arrested for DUI. He went on for thirty minutes, telling me how his life was empty and painful. Though he knew that God was calling him to a deeper walk, he did not think he could ever get there.

I started to offer sympathy for what he was feeling at the moment, but then I decided to change my tactic in counseling him. I said, "Well, you really stink. I mean, I can't tell you how much you really stink right now. You are finally getting what you deserve! You will never get any better at this. Everyone is disappointed in you, and there is no way to ever redeem yourself. God is disappointed....I am disappointed....And it will never be any different than that."

The silence on the phone was deafening. I waited for all of those thoughts to sink in. Then I said, "OK, are we done with all of those thoughts now?" His sigh of relief told me that he got the point. I went on to remind him, "Therefore, there is now no condemnation for those who are in Christ Jesus" (Romans 8:1 NIV). Yes, he would suffer the consequences of his sins on this planet, but God did not condemn him and neither would I. He did not need a self-righteous, "elder son" lecture on drinking and partying and how that was bad. He came to me fully aware of that. My job was to exhort him in the faith. To spur him on to good works and the way forward, not to focus on things behind and the "sin that so easily entangles" (Hebrews 12:1 NIV).

He needed to be reminded that we, as Christians, are the righteousness of God, and are already seated at the right hand of the Father! That is the grace of God that teaches us to say no to ungodliness (see Titus 2:11-12). That is His kindness that leads us to repentance (see Romans 2:4). When we become agents of this good news, we will see Christians run away from their sin and return to Christ. We must teach that the light at the end of the tunnel is there if we will simply turn around.

When we encounter someone who has fallen into sin, our temptation is to scold that person by showing all of the dangers and destruction he or she will reap from what has been sown. This tactic of the lawgiver will produce one of two things: another self-righteous person who rededicates his or her life for the ninetieth time, thinking, *This time it will work*, or a person who feels condemned, disillusioned, and discouraged in his or her walk.

In contrast to the elder son, the loving father immediately threw open his arms and ran to the son. His acceptance for him was immediate. There was no probationary period. There was no conditional forgiveness or steps the father demanded the son go through before he would be allowed back into the graces of his father. He said, "My son has come home again!" Then he threw a party! Our God is a God of a thousand second chances.

I believe everyone reading these words has benefited from that particular characteristic of the Father's heart more times than we would like to admit. As a young man, I myself went away. I left my parents' home and embraced a world of sin. I indulged myself for a time and found myself surrounded by figurative swine and consuming their dregs.

When I finally came to my end, I had to physically return to my family. It was 3:00 a.m. when I called my father and said, "Dad, I'm tired. I want to come home." He told me that if he needed to, he would break into a U-Haul store and come move my things that night.

My father met me on my path and restored me to the family. Experiencing that forgiveness and acceptance allows me to look back at that time when I am counseling the wayward sons and daughters and help them home with compassion. Remembering when you were at your worst will always open your heart to serve others who need to feel the embrace of the Father's arms around them when they are at their lowest point.

Jesus said we are to forgive others just as we have been forgiven. Again I say this does not mean that we allow people to abuse us, or that we become enablers to those who have not genuinely made a decision to come out of the pigpen. But when there is real repentance in people's lives we should always be ready to encourage them. There should always be an open door.

At this point I do want to bring a word of encouragement to all of you self-righteous elder sons who may be reading this. I want you to know that the Father loves and accepts you too. In the parable we see the elder son become indignant because his father had accepted the younger son so quickly; he even referred to himself as a slave in his father's service, which would have been a deeply offensive slam to his father. With the wisdom of a sage, his father turned to him and said,

HE HEART OF THE FATHER

"*Tekon*." That word in the original language carries with it beautiful, loving sentiments. It's the equivalent of "my baby" or "my child." He then corrected his son's accusation of slave-like treatment by reminding him that he had split his estate between the brothers at the beginning of his brother's rebellious exit. In fact, as I've stated before, at that moment the father owned nothing. He had given everything to his two sons when he "*divided his property between them*." He had lovingly, sacrificially given everything to both of them, but the older son did not see this as a free gift. He was still, in his mind, working for the father's love, grace, and inheritance. Because of this he felt like he *deserved* these things. He did not understand that both sons were being blessed far beyond what they deserved simply because of the father's amazing love for them. The father went on to lovingly inform his self-righteous son that they were no longer playing "the good boy/bad boy game" anymore. They were playing "the resurrection game"! He said, "My son was dead, and is alive again." How amazing that the father showed patience and acceptance to the older, ungrateful child as well as to the younger one. That's great news for those of you who have fallen into the trap of the elder son. Know that God loves you *for no good reason* as well.

So, among all of the lessons Jesus was teaching us in this parable, what can we learn about our actions as agents of God's love in this sometimes ungrateful, sinful world? Scripture says, "Out of the abundance of the heart the mouth speaks" (Matthew 12:34). Because God is expressing

Himself through our hearts to the world with an abundance of love, care, forgiveness, grace, and joy, my heart should be expressing God's heart to the world. The amount of love and grace that we can share is overwhelming. "They will know us by our love" is only the beginning. They should know us by the abundance of this extravagant love poured through our willing hearts to others by the power of the Holy Spirit. Just when I think I've expended all the love, grace, and forgiveness that I have to offer someone, there is more love, grace, and forgiveness in me. It can only come from the Father's heart expressed through me.

So we, as children of this loving "prodigal" Father, have an incredible message to share and live out to the world.

To the lost coins of the world, we say, "There is an extravagantly loving Savior who will never stop searching for you and He's ready to celebrate when you return."

To the lost sheep: "The good Shepherd will do whatever He must to bring you back into the fold."

And to the wayward sons and daughters we say, "Your Father accepts you, loves you, and will take you back the moment you return to Him. He has never lost sight of you, and if you come home, He will restore you."

Knowing our Father's heart toward all of us should spur us on to pour out this kind of grace on all those around us. But you still might be thinking that this task of living our lives totally spent for others is just too big an ask. So in the next two chapters we will look closer at two others who can serve as examples.

So What?

Meditate on the following Scripture.

> See what kind of love the Father has given to us, that
> we should be called children of God; and so we are.
> (1 John 3:1)

Do you ever focus on your own sin and find yourself
feeling condemned or not accepted by God? If so, read
the following passages and state them in your own words,
allowing the truth to "set you free."

Romans 5:1-21

Romans 8:1-4

Ephesians 2:8-13

- In the beginning of chapter 6 during the discussion of the three parables, I explained that Jesus never intended for His audience to focus on the lostness of the coin, the sheep, or the son. Jesus wanted us to see the loving, giving heart of the extravagant woman, the loving shepherd, and the prodigal father. In light of this, do you find yourself sometimes judgmental of those who have fallen away from their walk? Are you focused more on the why and how of their lostness than on seeing them repent and come home? If so write about that experience below.

- How have you experienced the lavishingly giving heart of our Heavenly Father?

- When Jesus said "It is finished!" on the cross, what does that mean in regard to your life and relationship to God today? What did Jesus provide for all His followers at that moment?

- Why do you think Christians have a difficult time offering unconditional love to those who have rebelled or walked away from their commitment to Christ? Why do you think we need to put that person who walked away "on probation"?

- Did you ever go through a time of "rebellion"?
  What brought you back to your walk with
  Christ?

- Have you ever found yourself in the shoes of the
  elder brother of the prodigal son, jealous of the
  blessings of a brother? Journal more about that
  time.

- Have you ever thought you were "slaving" for
  God, with no reward, as did the elder brother?
  Were you then reminded of God's love for you?
  If so, thank Him for His lavish love.

- Who do you relate with more today, the way-ward prodigal son or his elder brother? Why?

- What do you need to repent of if you have found a similarity to one of them? The rebellious spirit of the younger? the self-righteousness of the elder?

Pray and ask God to transform you by the renewing of your mind. Ask Him to help you pour love, forgiveness, and "prodigal grace" on others around you. And if you find this grace hard to accept yourself, ask the Lord to continue to reveal His heart to you.

- What is your one main takeaway from this chapter?

Now What?

This may be one of the toughest "Now What" sections yet: write down the name of someone who needs to know the prodigal, lavish, forgiving, and restoring heart of our heavenly Father (even if it is someone who has walked away from you, as well as his or her walk with God).

Make a plan to reconnect with that person and get him or her "back in your graces" with open arms and no conditions. *A word of caution: as has been stated before, this should not apply to those people who have been a part of an abusive or dangerous situation in your life.*

Ask the Lord for wisdom as you enter into this relationship and ask for guidance if needed from your local minister or a trusted mentor.

Chapter Seven

THE LIFE OF THE SON

But it shall not be so among you. But whoever would be great among you must be your servant, and whoever would be first among you must be slave of all. For even the Son of Man came not to be served but to serve, and to give his life as a ransom for many.
Mark 10:43-45

O f all the requests I make of God on a daily basis, I believe the most important is when I ask Him for wisdom. That's because the definition of wisdom is God's perspective. God has a helicopter view of time. He stands above it all and sees all of life, the motives, and the hearts of mankind. He can take in the past, present, and future of the universe at a glance. We want and need that perspective every day as we deal with the people around us. In fact, I believe that wisdom is the most vital gift God gives His children so they can see others as He does. That's why we looked at the heart of the Father in the last chapter. So I think it's fitting that we now see how that wisdom and grace was poured out to others in the life of the Son.

It goes without saying that Jesus is the ultimate guide to living *another life*. So let's look back at how He lived His few years here "in the flesh," funneling to us all that our Father had given Him. When we do this, we will see how Jesus embodied and modeled for us the most important and most difficult trait necessary to truly spend our lives for the sake of others: humility.

It always makes me smile when I observe church Christmas and Easter programs. We never have difficulty portraying the majesty and miracles of Jesus through huge productions with lights, fog machines, and thunderous musical scores. However, we seem to have a really hard time portraying His humbleness and servant's heart. Even when we represent Him in His meek, lowly entrance on to the earth in the stable, we fall to the grandiose temptation to end the scene with hosts of "angels" on wires and three elaborately dressed kings entering to blasts of trumpets and a finale of unfurling kingly robes that stretch all the way to the third pew!

Jesus could have chosen to enter history by being born to a royal family with influence and the political power to impact the world He came to, but He chose a carpenter and a virgin as His earthly parents. What a non-flamboyant, unassuming beginning!

Even His first miracle was done not for the amazement of the masses, but at the request of and out of respect for His mother. He turned the water into wine because His mother pressed Him with the concern that their host would be embarrassed at having run out of wine, not because He wanted to perform a party trick. In fact, Jesus did this before He even wanted to out Himself as a miracle-working Savior. He expressly told His mother, "My hour has not yet come" (John 2:4); still, He heard her plea and met the need.

He had arrived on the planet to introduce the world to the kingdom of God and to bring salvation, forgiveness, and grace to all mankind, but He was humble and loving enough to stop and meet the small needs of one…just one.

Another One and Another One… and Another One

He came for the many. He taught thousands on the hillsides. He preached in the synagogues, and throngs of people followed Him, but He never neglected the opportunity to minister to the one He saw who needed a special touch or word.

The woman with the issue of blood in Matthew 9 touched Him when throngs of people were clamoring to get a touch from Him. Though He was on His way to see to a synagogue leader's daughter, who had just died, He did not hesitate to stop and change this woman's life right there in the middle of the street.

Though He preached and taught the multitudes, He stopped and…

- called Zacchaeus out of the tree (Luke 19:1-10);

- offered the truth to the rich young ruler (Matthew 19:16-26);

- extended the possibility of a new life to the adulteress (John 8:1-11);

- healed the blind man (John 9:1-7); and

- had a cup of water with and restored the Samaritan woman (John 4:6-26).

All these things were done outside of any spotlight, with no accolades or even thanks in some cases. He left the glory of heaven to come to earth and minister to "the one." He did this as an example for us. Can you also humble yourself to minister with no expectation of accolades or applause?

When I was on the road with my interns going from conference to conference and event to event, I tried to develop this perspective within myself and instill it into these awesome guys. I reminded myself and them that we were not there just for the stage time. We needed to always be looking for "the one" who was in special need of prayers or attention. It never ceased to amaze us the people and circumstances God brought into our paths during those times. Oftentimes these "ones" showed up at the most inconvenient and difficult moments. That's when God taught us that serving others is costly, unheralded, sacrificial, and will usually mess up your plans. He lovingly reminded me to never become that speaker who blows into town with a polished, prepared message, who speaks and then immediately retreats to the hotel. Preparing a message for the masses is easier, in many ways, than answering questions and ministering to the deep needs of individuals. But those are the moments when true connection occurs and personal needs are met.

When we don't humble ourselves and relinquish our own agendas, we can miss the miracles that God is giving us the opportunity to partner with Him in.

Even at the moment of the greatest thing He ever did by dying on the cross, Jesus displayed His humility and His quiet servanthood.

"He was oppressed, and he was afflicted, yet he opened not his mouth: he is brought as a lamb to the slaughter, and as a sheep before her shearers is dumb, so he openeth not his mouth" (Isaiah 53:7 KJV).

That's just the way Jesus worked. He knew His purpose was to glorify the Father and not Himself. Through His silence, the power of God was released on the earth. God's power is everywhere we look, but it usually doesn't reveal itself in pomp and circumstance.

It is funny how the earth reveals the glory of the Lord and everything in it. When we think about the glory and power of God being expressed in nature, we think about majestic mountains, raging rivers, and the crashing waves of the sea. But God can be seen just as powerfully in the smallest details of life. Did you know that there can be up to six hundred pounds per square inch of pressure inside a walnut seed? In fact, a cocklebur seed can develop forces one thousand times the normal atmospheric pressure simply to break through its seed coat to germinate. Silent power and unseen miracles happen all around us.

As I mentioned earlier, I grew up in Florida. I can remember running outside the mall to see the space shuttles lift off from the Kennedy Space Center. To be present at a rocket launch is a thrilling experience. The power and sound of the rocket blasting off from its perch is breathtaking, but have you ever really thought about it? The culmination of all the technological knowledge of humans throughout the ages and all the power that we can muster can only make a pinprick in the silent gravitational pull and atmosphere of this planet. I wonder if it has made God smile to watch us and our feeble attempts at greatness. Silent power. That's just the way He prefers to work.

He became every detestable wretched act or motive that destroys the heart and soul of men...to destroy it for you.

On a recent trip to Haiti, our team saw God do seemingly small but amazing things, which is what always happens. Little things like...did we have enough nails? Yes, exactly the number to build a woman's roof—because we found an extra set in someone's work pouch. One day a love offering was spontaneously taken to buy some supplies at the last minute in a village. I found myself with an extra ten dollars at the end of my shopping spree and stuffed in my pocket, knowing God would show me how to use it. That afternoon the pastor and I went walking through the village to run an errand. We met a young boy working in the garden. The pastor asked why he wasn't in school, and the boy explained that his only pair of shoes were torn and he couldn't go to school without shoes. After telling him I would pray for him, I took about fifteen steps away from the house when God reminded me of what was in my shirt pocket. I walked back with a smile on my face, handed him the money, and told him to go buy shoes. The pastor turned to me with a tear in his eye and said, "God knew, didn't He?"

I shared this story that night with the team and explained how their generosity had been a blessing both for the school-children and for this one child in particular. A sweet woman spoke up from the back of the room and said that was just another "God wink." I had never heard that saying before, but now I look everywhere for the "God winks" of my life where God is quietly assuring me that He is there. Keep your eyes open! I can promise you that when you are attuned to the quiet ways God works and ask Him to reveal Himself to you, you'll see God winking throughout the day, in miracles He performs, and in the ones He gives you a chance to participate in.

Our God silently serves our needs every day. That's why He sent His Son on a silent night, a holy night, to humble parents in a humble stable, and announced His arrival to humble shepherds. Jesus became lower than the angels, an amazing act of humbleness. He left the throne, in a perfect place, with His perfect Father, to come to this broken, aching, and sin-filled planet to save us, the lowliest of all. However, He went way beyond this, beyond just coming to earth and being an example for us and ministering to the needs of those He met while He was here on earth. His last act for another was when He took your shame and guilt and mine and became our sin for us on the cross.

That's not just a concept to be understood. That is the crux of the gospel and why He came. Think about it. He served us. We rejected Him and still reject Him in many ways in our lives every day but...

> *He became sin for you.*
> *He became the greed you fell to last week.*
> *He became the lust you struggled with last*
> *night.*
> *He became murder.*
> *He became the lie you told your boss.*
> *He became the gossip you shared at school.*
> *He became every ungodly desire of your heart.*

For you.

He became every detestable wretched act or motive that destroys the heart and soul of men...to destroy it for you.

So what are you to do with that knowledge, and with that kind of a Savior? Knowing this should not only make us desire to walk in the righteousness He has given us, but it should also inspire us to live in humble selflessness. Knowing that Jesus loved us this much should move us to express this life to the world. Jesus's life should teach us to live humbly, serving all those around us with the grace and truth we have been given. We should not just preach these truths, but show others that they don't have to work for our love, that they can walk in our consistent, unconditional love. We should express to others that they do not owe us a debt, but that our forgiveness is freely given. We should show others our love by taking the time to stop and invest in their lives.

It is then that others will see God's truth fleshed out in us. Then they will truly understand. "For the grace of God has appeared that offers salvation to all people. It teaches us to say 'No' to ungodliness and worldly passions, and to live self-controlled, upright and godly lives in this present age, while we wait for the blessed hope—the appearing of the glory of our great God and Savior, Jesus Christ" (Titus 2:11-13 NIV).

These last two chapters may have been encouraging, but I know what some of you are thinking: *The Father and the Son poured their lives and hearts out for us, but I am not God and I am not Jesus. I am a simple, selfish human. How can I live like this?* Well, in the final chapter, we will examine the life of a simple man who did.

So What?

Meditate on the following Scripture.

> Have this mind among yourselves, which is yours in
> Christ Jesus, who, though he was in the form of God,
> did not count equality with God a thing to be grasped,
> but emptied himself, by taking the form of a servant,
> being born in the likeness of men. And being found in
> human form, he humbled himself by becoming obedient
> to the point of death, even death on a cross.
> (Philippians 2:5-8)

Paul told the Philippians that it was possible to "have" the
mind of Christ. This means Christians are given the privilege of access to God's perspective in all situations. Pray
and ask Jesus to give you His view of you. Ask Him to
open your eyes and heart to hear what He has to say about
your life.

- Think of someone you would consider Christ-like. What qualities does he or she possess that lead you to view them in that way?

- If humbleness is one of those qualities, how does he or she express that humbleness?

- List some costs to living a Christlike life.

- Describe a time in your life when someone let God change his or her plans to stop and minister to you or describe when God led you to do the same to someone else. What effect did this experience have on you?

- Have you ever experienced a God wink (a time when God performs the little miracles that go unnoticed and are rarely blatantly obvious)? Describe those times.

- Describe some ways God silently serves you every day? Take some time and thank Him for those things right now.

- How should Christ's humble service to man affect you daily?

Read Mark's description of the arrest, trial, crucifixion, and death of Jesus (see Mark 14–15). Note the number of times Jesus spoke. Stop and thank Jesus for His amazing restraint and the ultimate, humble act of silent sacrifice.

- Think of a situation you have experienced with someone that required a silent or sacrificial act of service. How did you respond? Are you experiencing one now? If so, how do you need to respond?

- Ask God to open your eyes this week to "the one." Write down different ways you can silently serve that person when no one is looking.

- What is your one main takeaway from this chapter?

Now What?

- Read 2 Corinthians 5:15-21 (emphasis on verse 21). Write in the space below some of the sins that Christ became for you on that cross. Close your eyes and thank Him for reconciling you to God (making you "right with God").

- Think of someone you may know who doesn't feel "right with God." Ask the Lord to show you how to be a minster of reconciliation in that person's life. Make a plan to "put feet to that prayer."

Chapter Eight

NOT JUST ANOTHER GUY

Humble yourselves, therefore, under the mighty hand of God
so that at the proper time he may exalt you, casting all your
anxieties on him, because he cares for you.
1 Peter 5:6-7

I have always believed all Christians should have someone in their lives whom they are mentoring and someone in their lives who is mentoring them. I believe that we improve through "holy envy." We see certain traits in people, and we want them for ourselves. This is one of the ways we grow. I also believe that the Lord placed in the Bible many people for us to study so that we might grow by their example. There are many bad examples for us to observe and learn from their mistakes, but there are several who lived exemplary lives that warrant not only our admiration but our emulation as well.

One such man is undoubtedly one of the most influential

and important disciples who ever lived, yet his influence was behind the scenes and his importance came through a humble, selfless heart. Most would never name him on any list of Bible characters. Very little is known about this amazing man, and fewer than thirty verses speak of his life and ministry, but his servant's heart and giving spirit shaped and defined the very meaning of the term *Christian*, and his impact can still be felt today.

Our job is to make the most of what we have for Him.

His name was Barnabas.

Though there is not much written about this unsung hero, his life is an amazing example of someone who poured his life out for another.

Through the years, Barnabas and his life have been tragically misrepresented by well-meaning teachers who use his life story to bring about conviction because they feel their students are not nice enough or members of their congregations are not encouraging one another. I've also heard this statement: "Thank you for the encouragement. You are my Barnabas." And though many amiable traits are definitely found in him, they only scratch the surface of the character of this man. He was not simply a sweet, timid, encouraging "yes-man" for the apostle Paul, as many portray him.

So let's delve a little deeper into his life and see if we might grow from "holy envy."

He Was a Generous Giver

First, we find that he was a generous *giver*. Acts 4:36-37 says, "Thus Joseph, who was also called by the apostles Barnabas (which means son of encouragement), a Levite, a native of Cyprus, sold a field that belonged to him and brought the money and laid it at the apostles' feet." Barnabas gave. He gave of his time, and he abundantly gave of his finances to fund Paul's ministry and the gospel that was being spread during the foundation of the church.

Many people who read this don't have the financial ability to fund great ministries. But all of us have a measure of time to invest. All of us possess gifts and talents that are unique to us that may be integral to the success and expanding of God's kingdom.

Though Scripture lists spiritual gifts given by God, I believe many obvious gifts were not listed, gifts such as writing, acting, and athleticism. I believe these are also gifts given by God for the purpose of expanding His kingdom. Our job is to make the most of what we have for Him. We serve Him more when we grow and enhance our own talents in order to give back to the church and those around us. If your pastor has the gift of preaching, it is not outrageous for you to expect him or her to grow and expand that gift as a communicator. We expect musicians to practice and rehearse in order to offer their very best to God. Administrators, evangelists, and youth ministers should all be improving their talents. We expect and should demand that they learn more about their crafts so that they will impact God's kingdom to the greatest extent of their abilities.

When givers learn the joys and blessings of sacrificial giving, the kingdom of God benefits, but so does the giver. They find peace and purpose, accomplishment, and a feeling of legacy to be a part of something meaningful and eternal.

Once again, though, I must warn those who are generous givers. One of the pitfalls of generous giving is to fall to the temptation of "ownership." Ownership occurs when the giver determines that, because he or she is a major funder of the organization, he or she has the right to direct that ministry and its operations. That "right" belongs only to God.

I would say to those who feel that way about giving: just as the ministers and administrators of an organization do not have the right to tell you how to make or spend the resources God has entrusted you with, you should allow them the right to use their gifts of leadership to run the organizations God has assigned to them.

He Was a Generous Receiver

Second, we learn that Barnabas was a generous *receiver*. Acts 11:24 says, "For he was a good man, full of the Holy Spirit and of faith. And a great many people were added to the Lord."

I believe Barnabas's generosity was motivated by the fact that he knew that he had already received so much. He had received salvation, which in and of itself is the greatest gift anyone can receive. The Scriptures tell us he was full of the Holy Spirit. Therefore, I believe he gave knowing he had already received from the Lord. He lived to be an example. The generosity of God toward His children is sometimes taken for granted, but Barnabas did not take that generosity for granted. Instead, he gave abundantly as an example for others to do the same.

Ephesians 1:7-9 says, "In him we have redemption through his blood, the forgiveness of sins, in accordance with the riches of God's grace that he lavished on us. With all wisdom and understanding, he made known to us the mystery of his will according to his good pleasure, which he purposed in Christ" (NIV).

Do you see this? God has given us *everything* we need! That's quite an impressive gift list. On top of this, to many of us He adds health, financial blessings, and the very air we breathe. All of these prove that we are pampered by our loving Father and as abundant receivers, giving should be a natural outpouring.

He Was a Humble Leader

Next we find that Barnabas was a *humble leader*. Acts 11:26 tells us, "And when he had found him, he brought him to Antioch. For a whole year they met with the church and taught a great many people. And in Antioch the disciples were first called Christians."

In the early church writings, there was a common practice

of listing a group of people by their order of importance. Pay attention to the times the apostles were listed. The list always went Peter, James, and John…and then some other guys I always felt sorry for because they weren't listed. In recounting the events of Acts, and particularly the beginnings of the ministry of Paul and Barnabas, Barnabas is always listed first.

> Acts 11:26: "Barnabas and Saul met with the church…" (NIV)
>
> Acts 12:25: "When Barnabas and Saul had finished their mission…" (NIV)
>
> Acts 13:2: "Set apart for me Barnabas and Saul…" (NIV)

Barnabas was obviously deemed the more important of the two. He was well known to the churches of that day. It seems many held him in great esteem and people respected him. They knew his reputation as a good man. But a curious thing occurs in Acts 13:42, when Paul began to speak in the synagogues. He gained his own reputation as a true apostle. From then on, Barnabas is no longer listed first.

> Acts 13:42: "As Paul and Barnabas were leaving the synagogue…" (NIV)
>
> Acts 14:23: "Paul and Barnabas appointed elders…" (NIV)

Barnabas, who was a highly respected man, humbled himself and took a back seat to Paul's ministry. To this day, we refer to the early missionary journeys as Paul's. Truthfully, those first missionary journeys were Barnabas's. He was the person known and respected by the churches. Paul's reputation, if known at all, was that of a murderer and persecutor of Christians. But in time, as Paul's influence expanded, Barnabas humbled himself and took a supporting role to the ministry of Paul.

In today's world, we stress leadership skills. Millions of dollars are spent every year by corporations and churches to train leaders. How many "Follower" conferences have you heard of? No, I didn't think so. I submit the reason is because no one wants to take a support role. We want to be Paul, not Barnabas.

As I have traveled over the last two decades, though I am the face or at least the mouth of our ministry, I have never worked alone. I have an incredible staff that serves with me, who receive no public praise for their work. We would never be able to accomplish all that our ministry does on a weekly basis without the skill and humble leadership of these remarkable men and women in the areas of our organization in which they serve.

Barnabas's leadership style would fly in the face of most of today's teachings about leadership. Yet Barnabas's influence and ministry were massive. Acts 11:22 tells us that Barnabas became the pastor of what would eventually become the first megachurch in the world, boasting thousands of members. Yet we do not have one written word of a message he ever spoke. That is an example of what I believe was his humble, quiet, servant leadership style. He influenced thousands, just as Paul did, but never received the recognition that Paul enjoyed. Everyone wants to be Paul, but ministries fall without the Barnabases as well.

One of my first jobs at a church was as assistant director of the Christian Life Center of a large church. My jobs included passing out basketballs and skates and sweeping the gym floor. For years, I wore many other hats at that church. I directed musicals and special events. Because of this, I was often stretched pretty thin and would often need help. That is when I called one of the volunteers I knew I could trust. One of those volunteers was a man I'll refer to as Mr. Bob, because he would never want the attention. That was the kind of man he was.

Mr. Bob could be called on to help mow lawns, construct play sets, or even take charge of the front desk at the gym. I remember many conversations with Mr. Bob that went like this: "Mr. Bob, can you clean the skates?" "Mr. Bob, can you paint the underside of that railing?" "Mr. Bob, would you mind folding the towels today?" His response was always the same: "Whatever you need, Brent."

Then came the Memorial Day church service when our church honored its veterans and active military. Mr. Bob walked down the aisle in his full dress uniform carrying the American flag, and for the first time I saw who he really was. He wasn't Mr. Bob at all. He was a retired high-ranking military officer. Thousands of men and women had saluted him as he gave orders and deployed men and women all around the world. At that moment, memories flashed through my head: *Mr. Bob, could you take out the trash for me? Mr. Bob, can you spray disinfectant in the showers and change out the toilet paper?*

What a humble leader Mr. Bob was! He was a man we could all learn lessons from. He exemplified so many of the traits we have discussed in this book. He truly lived another kind of life. He will forever be a Barnabas to me.

He Was an Encouraging Comforter

Barnabas was also an *encouraging comforter*. The very name *Barnabas* literally means "encouragement," and encouragement and exhortation defined his life. In Acts 11:22-24, he exhorted the believers. I know the value of a great exhorter. Ms. Verhagen, my fifth-grade teacher, was a very harsh woman to many people. She was a boisterous and passionate woman. Many of my classmates never liked her. In fact, I had a chair in her closet because I was placed there so often for talking too much. (Shocker!) However, when so many people saw my hyperactivity as a discipline problem, she saw it as creativity. I will never forget the words she said to me on my last day in her class: "I will see you graduate with honors and go on to great things." Although she passed away before my graduation, I made it a point to visit her grave shortly after to thank her. Her words remain with me to this day. She saw the potential in me that others missed.

Encouragement should never be confused with flattery or a simple compliment. Just as the word *enthrone* means to put on the throne, *encourage* means to place courage in someone. Barnabas understood that. When no one saw the potential in Paul, Barnabas did. Through his words and deeds, Barnabas encouraged Paul to become great. It seems to be apparent in the Scriptures that Barnabas also infused courage in the people of Antioch and the many churches he and Paul began and supported (see Acts 13:43; 15:35).

It is worthy to note that though Barnabas was an uplifting source of strength to the people around him, it did not mean in any way that he was timid. He apparently was not afraid to confront and correct people when he saw them straying from the faith. In Acts 13, Barnabas and Paul confronted Jewish leaders. In 14:8-18, Barnabas joined Paul again in confronting the people of Lystra about false gods and idol worship. The people wanted to worship the two of them!

To encourage someone to come back to the well-worn paths of the narrow road when they stray from their walk is also a way to serve them. So encouragement can take on many facets.

He was a Consistent Risk-Taker

As with most of Barnabas's character, these two attributes seem to be polar opposites, but as we will see, they blended perfectly in this man.

Acts 12:25 states, "And Barnabas and Saul returned

from Jerusalem when they had completed their service." Barnabas seems to be a man who stayed consistent to his beliefs and his calling, no matter how much opposition and hardship he had to endure. This was a steady, levelheaded man who was determined to finish the work. I wonder if he realized how much he was living out the example of Christ to those he ministered to. Remember what Jesus said: "My food is to do the will of him who sent me and to accomplish his work" (John 4:34). How fulfilled and satisfied he must have been!

When I was a toddler, I stood on the diving board shivering with fear as my father treaded water in the deep end of the swimming pool below me. I can't imagine how tired he must've been, hearing me ask the same question over and over: "Daddy, are you going to catch me?" "Daddy, are you going to catch me?" "Daddy, are you *sure* you're going to catch me?"

When I finally jumped and felt my father's arms around me holding me up, I gained the confidence to jump again and again, never having to repeat the question, "Are you going to catch me?" As I grew into manhood, my father caught me many times as I fell into the deep end of situations. I never felt like I would drown, knowing that I had a consistent father who would catch me every time I fell or got in over my head.

When we think about spending our lives in the service of others, the skills of consistent friendship and reliability are important to cultivate. Encouragement should be more than just flattering words, though. Remember, if you say you will catch them, then you gotta catch them. Your deeds will always speak louder than your words.

Barnabas was a constant source of love, encouragement, and investment in those around him. He believed in Paul and saw something in him when no one else did. He risked his reputation with the churches he was associated with by asking them to allow Paul to teach them. Throughout Paul's early ministry he could always count on Barnabas to have his back. This solid partnership paid off, evidenced by the spreading of the gospel across the Middle East.

But Barnabas's consistency seemed to backfire when he applied the same philosophy to his young cousin/intern John Mark.

> And after some days Paul said to Barnabas, "Let us return and visit the brothers in every city where we proclaimed the word of the Lord, and see how they are." Now Barnabas wanted to take with them John called Mark. But Paul thought best not to take with them one who had withdrawn from them in Pamphylia and had not gone with them to the work. And there arose a sharp disagreement, so that they separated from each other. Barnabas took Mark with him and sailed away to Cyprus, but Paul chose Silas and departed, having been commended by the brothers to the grace of the Lord. And he went through Syria and Cilicia, strengthening the churches. (Acts 15:36-41)

Barnabas saw something great within the heart of the scribe John Mark. Though Mark was young and full of fear, Barnabas was not the type of man to give up on someone. It's astonishing that Paul seemed to lose faith in someone so quickly. I have often imagined the argument that day between Paul and Barnabas:

> **Paul:** *"Now, do you really think that's wise, Barnabas? We have an important task and don't have time for second chances."*
> **Barnabas:** *"Oh, God would never want us to give someone a second chance, Saul…I mean, Paul! Aren't you the poster child for second chances?"*

I think things may have gone downhill from there.

Sometimes our risks with people don't seem to pay off. As a result of the disagreement between Paul and Barnabas, a remarkable thing happened. Acts 15 says they had such a sharp disagreement that they parted company.

The other effect of this split between Paul and Barnabas was that John Mark continued to be discipled by Barnabas. History tells us that John Mark returned to Jerusalem, where he later worked

We gain our lives by losing them.

for a man named Peter. Peter was so impressed with John Mark that he gave him a great honor. Seeing the servant spirit of this disciple of Barnabas, he asked John Mark to be his scribe, to write a retelling of the life of Jesus as Peter experienced it. Because of this, we have the wonderful Gospel of Mark, where we see Jesus through the eyes of a humbled, discipled servant.

Even Paul came around and affirmed the ministry of Mark. In 2 Timothy 4:11, he wrote, "Get Mark and bring him with you, for he is very useful to me for ministry." If it had not been for Barnabas pouring his life into a young intern named Mark, we would lack the vital perspective of Christ as the suffering servant that only a true servant would see. So Barnabas's risk paid off. And it paid off for all of us.

He Was a Genuine Christian

One of the things I love the most about this man Barnabas was that he was genuine and real. Not only does the argument with Paul prove his human imperfection, but in Galatians 2:13, we see him fall. Christians, even wonderful men and women of God, can let pride and temptation get in their way. Barnabas was not immune to failure. This makes him real and even relatable as a role model to men and women.

The biggest impact Barnabas had on the world was simply by being an authentic servant of God. And though the accomplishments of this disciple would be enough for a lifetime, Barnabas gave us something else, something earth shattering, and again he did it in a humble, behind-the-scenes way.

Acts 11:26b: "And in Antioch the disciples were first called Christians."

The word *Christian*, which means "little Christ," was first invented as a derogatory term to describe followers of Jesus and His teachings. These fanatics lived communally, giving to the poor and feeding the sick. They were touching the unclean and serving "the least of these." This was completely contrary to the selfish culture of that day. But how did they follow Jesus's way so passionately? They never met Jesus in the flesh or heard his teachings. They were Christlike because of the example of their mentor/pastor. Barnabas's most amazing contribution to Christianity is the word *Christian* itself. That's the power of *another life*.

In keeping with the true definition of a Christian, we are to be ambassadors of Christ in this world. As Barnabas reflected the life of Christ to those around him, we are to do the same today. This is what makes us aliens and strangers. We are to forgive one another. We are to live in community, submitting to one another, loving one another, bearing with one another until His return. Even though it may seem crazy to the world, the truth is, the upside-down kingdom is the only right and fulfilling way to live. We gain our lives by losing them. We are refreshed every day with living water as we let it flow through us to others. We utterly spend ourselves for the cause of Christ, knowing our fulfillment comes only from Him.

So What?

Meditate on the following Scripture.

> Humble yourselves, therefore, under the mighty hand of God so that at the proper time he may exalt you, casting all your anxieties on him, because he cares for you. (1 Peter 5:6-7)

- How much did you know about Barnabas before this chapter? Had you ever considered him an important disciple? Why or why not?

- Barnabas was a generous person. Write below some of the ways he gave of himself, his life, and his resources.

- Would you consider yourself a leader like Paul or a supportive, behind-the-scenes person? What are your feelings about your perceived role?

- Take a moment and write down a few people in your past who encouraged you and spurred you on in some way. Think about your interactions with them. Were they always positive? Were they sometimes confrontational? How were these people different from one another? What were the consistencies in the way they treated you and what can you learn from them?

- Have you ever taken a risk to invest in someone and that person failed? How did you respond?

- Have you ever failed someone else who invested in you?

- Are you now investing your life in someone? In what ways are you investing your life in that person?

- Is someone mentoring you now? If the answer is no, in what areas of your life would you say you need a mentor? a financial advisor? a spiritual mentor? someone to help you become better in your career or in your relationships?

- What is hindering you from pouring your life into someone now?

- What is hindering you from finding a mentor yourself?

- What is your one main takeaway from this chapter?

Now What?

The "Now What?" for this final chapter is obvious. If you are not being mentored and mentoring someone, ask God to identify those people. Seek out the people that God would have you invest in and those you want to invest in you.

OH, AND ANOTHER THING

Because of the increase of wickedness,
the love of most will grow cold.
Matthew 24:12 NIV

I believe the timing of this book's release is a "God thing." In the verse above, Jesus was warning His followers to prepare for the last days. I'm not prophesying Jesus's return within the next month or even year, but each day that passes is obviously one day closer to those end days. As the world grows colder, we who represent the heart of Christ have an amazing opportunity to stand as warm beacons of God's love.

The light shines in the darkness, and the
darkness has not overcome it. (John 1:5)

Have you ever walked into a room that was completely dark and turned on a flashlight? Where did the darkness go?

Does it go hide in a corner? Does it cower under the bed? No. Light overcomes, it dispels the darkness. In the same way as we pour ourselves out to others, we overcome the darkness around us. Servanthood overcomes hate. It overcomes prejudice and can disarm our enemies. As Christians, this sacrificial love is our best weapon in this darkened world. Just as Paul, in describing the downfall of man, said, "But where sin increased, grace abounded all the more" (Romans 5:20b). In these times of sin abounding more and more on the planet, people of grace and deeds of grace should abound as well.

Now if, at the end of this book, you are thinking that this living-for-another thing is too hard to keep up, is too hard to maintain 24/7, then you are correct. To live the perfect Christian life of complete humility and servanthood is not difficult...it's impossible. It's been said that the only guy to ever live the perfect Christian life was crucified, and that's true. We cannot live the perfect life. Only Jesus could do that.

But we are called to be an example of His life and live in a way that points others to Jesus by our modeling of His character and love. So how do you do it? Let me calm your fear of failure. Remember in the first chapter we discussed that Christ already set us up for victory because of this truth: "I am the vine; you are the branches"? You don't have to do it in your own power. He intends for you to simply let Him live His life through you. Remember when Paul said "...and Christ, who is your life." This is what he was trying to explain.

One of the most wonderful things about Christianity is that we are the only religion where its followers don't have to try hard and work ourselves to death straining and toiling to be like our God. One of the most wonderful benefits of Christianity is that our Savior inhabits us! He gives more than just a ticket to heaven: He gives us; He grants us power for living a life that is honoring to Him today!

I don't have to perform for my God. I only need to allow Him to express His life in me. This does not, however, happen overnight. It's a lifelong journey. As you daily meditate on Him and His words, then His Spirit, His mind, and His thoughts permeate yours and make of you so much more than you could ever be by yourself. He wants to love another, bear with another, forgive another through you.

His intent is not merely to help us live this life but also to make less of us and more of Him. Then we can stand with people like Paul, Barnabas, and all the "little Christs" who have gone before us and say, "To live is Christ and to die is gain."

I hope that this is a relief and that a weight has been lifted off your shoulders. However, let me give you a tip, a helpful mind-set that I think will encourage you to *live for another* tomorrow. As we've learned, Christians represent Christ to the world. However, the Bible clearly teaches us that all people are made in God's image. That's an amazing gift from God to all mankind but it is especially useful to those of us who serve Him here as our Lord. Why? Because it makes our service to others simply an extension of our worship of God! The next time you need to bear with someone, submit to someone, or love someone, see that person first as being made in the image of God. The next time you get into a disagreement with someone, see that person first as the image of God. The next time you see an enemy, see that person first as the image of God. Then serve your God by treating them in a way that honors that image of your God. Just as God sees His reflection in you, you should see God's reflection in the people you deal with on a daily basis as you serve them.

My hope is that you have been encouraged by this book and, like me, that you will latch onto these truths and begin to see the incredible fulfillment and joy that spending yourself for others can bring to you. The abundant life Jesus promised us is not simply available to you, it is the natural state of a true Christian. Just remember that you were made to be a branch in the vine of Christ that bears fruit. Let the roots run deep in Him and let Him live ANOTHER life through you.